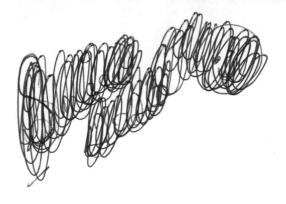

The Reluctant Disciple
Daring to Believe

David Wells

D0829652

NOVALIS

Copyright © Redemptorist Publications 2015

The moral right of David Wells to be identified as the author of this work has been asserted in accordance with the *Copyright, Designs and Patents Act 1988.*

Nihil Obstat: Fr Michael Wheaton (Censor Deputatus)
Imprimatur: Bishop Mark O'Toole (Bishop of Plymouth)

Designed by Peena Lad
Photo of the author by Mark Wayer

Published in Canada by Novalis

Publishing Office   Head Office
10 Lower Spadina Avenue, Suite 400   4475 Frontenac Street
Toronto, Ontario, Canada   Montréal, Québec, Canada
M5V 2Z2   H2H 2S2

www.novalis.ca

Cataloguing in Publication is available from Library and Archives Canada

Published in the United Kingdom by Redemptorist Publications
Alphonsus House, Chawton, Hampshire, GU34 3HQ, UK
Tel. +44 (0)1420 88222, Fax. +44 (0)1420 88805
Email rp@rpbooks.co.uk, www.rpbooks.co.uk
A registered charity limited by guarantee
Registered in England 3261721

Printed in Canada.

All rights reserved. No part of this publication may be reproduced, stored in a retrieval system, or transmitted in any form, or by any means, electronic, mechanical, photocopying, recording, or otherwise, without prior written permission from Redemptorist Publications.

The publisher gratefully acknowledges permission to use the following copyright material:

Excerpts from the New Revised Standard Version of the Bible: Anglicised Edition, © 1989. 1995, Division of Christian Education of the National Council of the Churches of Christ in the United States of America. Used by permission. All rights reserved.

Surprised by Joy by C. S. Lewis, copyright © C. S. Lewis Pte. Ltd, 1955. Extract reprinted by permission.

We acknowledge the financial support of the Government of Canada through the Canada Book Fund for business development activities.

5   4   3   2   22   21   20   19   18

In fact there are innumerable events in life and human situations which offer the opportunity for a discreet but incisive statement of what the Lord has to say in this or that particular circumstance. It suffices to have true spiritual sensitivity for reading God's message in events.

Evangelii Nuntiandi, 43

Today too, people prefer to listen to witnesses: they "thirst for authenticity" and "call for evangelizers to speak of a God whom they themselves know and are familiar with, as if they were seeing him".

Evangelii Gaudium, 150

David writes with a passion for living his everyday life with richness and colour. I love his stories because they move me, make me laugh and are underpinned with a deep love of God and God's world. His experience as an educator leads him to understand what matters to ordinary people. His open and honest reflections about scripture and his faith are refreshing, imaginative and at times quite surreal. Yet overall, his humanity shines through his writing and the practical comments and questions that conclude each story root this book in the real world. I know many of my Anglican colleagues, lay and ordained, would enjoy his approach and I shall certainly recommend this to them.

Reverend Canon Dr Graham M. Dodds MA
Canon Treasurer, Wells Cathedral and Director of Learning Communities (Bath & Wells Diocese)

With self-deprecating humour, David tells gentle stories that describe a powerful Spirit at work in his life. Reading a story a day might gently awaken that same Spirit in the life of the reader. I and many others have been enchanted by hearing him speak so I'm delighted that his storytelling gift is now available to a wider audience.

Fr Christopher Jamison OSB
Director, National Office for Vocation, Catholic Bishops' Conference of England and Wales

If Christianity works, it is not confined to sacred space but lives happily in the ordinary space of people's lives. David Wells inhabits ordinary space with extraordinary insight. He anchors the beauty of the Gospel in the high street, in the market place, in the home, in the school, in the wonderful muddle and mix of ordinary time. The world of every day is where we live; there is nowhere else to live the Gospel. In this book you are invited to listen to a master storyteller uncover the beauty of ordinary time.

Where you live, where you struggle, he says, there is Gospel. Surely that is Good News indeed!
Fr Denis McBride CSsR

Those who have had the joy of hearing David Wells speak will know what it means to be excited and encouraged by their Catholic faith. Thankfully, anyone who reads this book can get to know David, be spiritually uplifted, and feel happy being just as God made them.
Most Reverend Malcolm McMahon, Archbishop of Liverpool

David Wells has captured the power of Jesus' storytelling in an imaginative way. He does so in his own inimitable and accessible way, and I am sure this book of reflections will help many in their own following of Jesus Christ.
Right Reverend Mark O'Toole, Bishop of Plymouth

We shall only be able to share our faith if we touch people's imagination. David Wells' stories do just this. They are wonderfully honest, often amusing, and always profound. This is a book from which everyone can benefit, from the seasoned preacher to the tentative inquirer.
Fr Timothy Radcliffe OP

In this kaleidoscope of reflections, David Wells demonstrates wit and wisdom as sacred truths blossom out of the most ordinary scenes. A collection of contemporary parables written by a reluctant disciple, these delightfully observed episodes are a blessing and will live long in the mind. By linking each meditation to a Gospel passage, the reader is at once charmed and cajoled into seeing differently, thinking differently and acting differently. Highly recommended.
Dr Anthony Towey, the Aquinas Centre, St Mary's University, Twickenham

About the author

David began his career as a teacher working with reluctant teenagers. There he learned how to teach young people who were bored easily and who expected religion to be constraining. It turned out to be good training for adult education as well. "These days," he says, "if you have a spiritual inclination, some people expect you to be stupid, dull, extremist or creepy. In a world of special effects and virtual reality, making the things of God relevant and real is a greater challenge than ever."

David spends most of his working hours in a converted farm building in the grounds of Buckfast Abbey. His task alongside a small, dedicated team is to encourage opportunities for adults to grow in faith and confidence and become witnesses of God's love. He calls it helping people to move beyond their reluctance.

Along with his work in England, David has spoken at over three hundred conferences around the world, mainly to teachers. Venues he has spoken in range from arenas holding thousands, to small groups in musty parish halls. He approaches both with equal enthusiasm.

David guest-lectures in three universities and is passionately committed to education. His hope is to renew a sense of nobility in the teaching profession: "We have given ourselves to performance," he says, "whereas the art of teaching is a much richer, more exciting and holier task than proving ourselves 'good' or 'outstanding.'"

When he's not working, you'll catch him messing about on the River Exe in Devon or watching Sam, Matt or Emily play sport. Alison, David's long-suffering wife, features in many of his stories – and invariably comes out of them better than he does. When this book is written he has promised Alison he will buy a new pair of running shoes and look at them daily. He has also promised to divorce his laptop, which is the third party in their relationship.

Acknowledgments

For my parents, Margaret and John, who showed me how to love, for Alison, who loves me despite my laptop, and for Sam, Matt and Emily, who have never been brought home in a police car (as at the time of writing).

With thanks to the many gifted colleagues I have worked with over the years in the Briars at Crich, St John Houghton School, the CES, the Nottingham Diocese and the Plymouth Diocese. Thanks also to the team at Redemptorist Publications for making this book happen, especially my editor Caroline for her attention to tenses, apostrophes and deadlines (three things I struggle to love at all), and to Fr Michael Wheaton for his careful scrutiny.

Dedication

During the course of writing this book I was aware of three young people who took their own lives. This book is dedicated to them and their families. A donation from the royalties of this book will go to charities who work with young people at risk and their families.

Contents

Introduction

In the Trinity Term of 1929 I gave in, and admitted that God was God, and knelt and prayed: perhaps, that night, the most dejected and reluctant convert in all England. I did not then see what is now the most shining and obvious thing; the Divine humility which will accept a convert even on such terms. The Prodigal Son at least walked home on his own feet. But who can duly adore that Love which will open the high gates to a prodigal who is brought in kicking, struggling, resentful, and darting his eyes in every direction for a chance of escape?

C. S. Lewis, *Surprised by Joy*

Why reluctant?

On a damp dreary night shrouded in orange lamplight, I walked to the university chapel and proceeded through the heavy oak doors and into the dark vast space beyond. The chapel was lit by a solitary flickering candle which appeared to animate the statues. Statues don't smile. They just stare accusingly, as if to condemn all the doubts in your mind. It was eerie. There was a feeling of being watched. What I was about to do had to be done alone, away from spying eyes. So I looked around. Checking and checking again that I had privacy, I turned to face the altar and the crucifix which hung before me. I was alone.

There were three reasons for being alone in that chapel. Firstly, there was the feeling I had picked up through my childhood that funny, popular, sporty people don't go in for church. Church people appeared to me to be a bit needy. When I used to listen to a sermon I would wonder if all this community spirit was being experienced by people in pubs rather than churches. To me, the people outside the Christian Union looked like they were having a better time than those in it. The last thing I was looking for was an alcohol-free party with no girls.

The second problem was more fundamental. My church experience seemed a bit pointless. There didn't seem to be much happening. Gathering over and over again to reflect, sing, or pray the liturgy didn't seem to be achieving a great deal. It struck me that the poor and vulnerable were better served by social workers than by Christianity, that the excluded were better championed by socially motivated groups, while the churches I knew were gazing at their own navels.

My final problem was to do with intellect. At university I had been challenged and provoked, not just by ideas but by the way other people lived. It struck me that some truly remarkable people were finding answers to their questions in places other than the Church. The growing confidence of science and the torrid history of religion made a case for postmodernism. The dominant philosophy at university was to choose your own truth. To do anything else was to have no mind of your own, to be indoctrinated.

For these three reasons, if I was to have a religious journey it would be something I'd do quietly, avoiding the judgement of my postmodern peers. If I was to be a disciple I'd be a reluctant, covert one.

Sitting there I was totally conflicted. Part of me was waiting to hear a voice out of the darkness. Another part of me was bemused at my being there at all. Part of me wanted to talk to a God I didn't know or understand and another part of me, the one in the student union bar with my friends, was asking, "What are you doing here, are you having some sort of crisis?"

There was no crisis, no broken heart, no abusive parents or desperate addiction. Behind me were nineteen happy years. It was difficult to know exactly what I was doing there. It was as if I had a question that needed an answer but I didn't even know what the question was. There was a restlessness that lived just below the surface of things. It was easy to distract myself from it, but in the quiet gaps between everything, I was left with the feeling that there had to be more to life than getting what I wanted. Coming here to this darkened sanctuary, I could almost indulge it, provoke it, wrestle with it, although I had no idea what "it" was.

Being in churches like this had been a feature of my upbringing. There was something very tired and habitual about my years of obligation. In church services I knew when to stand up, when to sit down, when to speak, when not to speak, and it all rolled out in front of me over and over again. Until one day, I start asking, "There is no one my age here. What am I doing here?"

As a child I had been baptised into something unknowingly – a promise made for me. It was not my promise. God, it seemed to me, had no grandchildren. Sitting in the chapel in February 1981 I knew where to start looking because of that very baptism, but now the search was up to me. I had little idea who I was really speaking to, what words to use or what I was trying to achieve. So I made a feeble bargain with God: "Lord," I said, not really knowing what the title meant, "if what they say about you is true, make yourself known to me." Then I went on to say something really reckless: "If this happens, you can have my life." It made sense to me. Surely if God is real then why chase after something else? But it was a naïve prayer. The question is often asked, what does a dog do if the car it is chasing stops? What would we do if God answered back?

There you have it, the most uneventful conversion story of all time. No lightning or voice inside me. God had answered my prayer but I didn't know it. Not yet. Leaving, I slipped back into the dreary fog much as I had slipped into the chapel. With collar up and my head down, you'd think I'd just walked out of a strip club rather than a holy place.

The stories in this book tell of a gradual awakening – a discovery that the God I had been looking for was there all the time. Already near. God would begin to reach me through all the ordinary mundane encounters that look like a life. My journey would become extraordinary, not because of what I did, but because of how I would begin to see the things that happened to me. What a happy discovery. God was waiting for me to overcome my reluctance. This book explores the many guises of that reluctance and how over time God would begin to help me move though them and beyond them. All I had to do was wait and see.

Why stories?

In the summer of 1994 I was about to give a keynote presentation at a conference venue in London. The conference was based upon two pieces of research, one conducted by me and another by a lecturer from a northern university. For two years I had been researching into the problems that Catholic schools were having recruiting teachers. After two years of interviews, careful scrutiny of other research and some reasonably sophisticated statistics, my paper was ready. To aid my presentation I had some animated graphics and meticulous handouts. All sorts of senior people would be there: bishops, government ministers and leaders from all levels of education. It was all set up for me: fresh cloths on the tables, sharpened pencils, water in bottles with marble stoppers, a dish with mints. Every dog has its day. This was mine.

In the few seconds at the lectern before I began to speak, I became acutely aware just how fortunate I was. Paid research is rare, and I had been given an opportunity to thoroughly investigate an issue which was of concern to all these people. In front of me were credible leaders about to dignify my work by listening to my speech. Sitting closest to me on the front row were my colleagues who had inspired me to be here. It was important to do well for the faith they had put in me. Taking a sharp intake of breath and gripping the lectern with both hands as if I needed it to support me, I began to read my paper. The sixty minutes went quickly. The paper provoked good questions and there was polite applause. Although I am never elated after a presentation, I was satisfied that it had gone well and I would enjoy my lunch.

As I was about to tuck into the delicious-looking dessert, one of the conference organisers approached me: "Do you mind if I have a brief word?" he said, ushering me away from the table. He seemed highly agitated: "It seems that the next keynote is unwell," he continued, gripping my wrist. "Do you have any more material?" His predicament was plain to see. He needed someone to cover the last-minute cancellation: "Would it be possible to take a few of the issues you have raised this morning and develop them further?" As I listened to his pleading I was aware just how carefully I had choreographed the previous session and practised it over and over again. Could I really go out there again, this time without a paper to hand?

"I'm not sure I have any more material," I said. "The data is evidenced in the report." The look on his face made me feel guilty. Wanting to help, I suggested an alternative: during the interviews I had met some remarkable people who told me stories about their lives. "Yes, yes, that sounds fascinating," he said, as if he would accept whatever I offered him. I tried to lower his expectations: "If you explain why I'm appearing a second time today, I'd be happy to offer a few reflections on some of the people I met who care about these issues." It was all he needed. Before I'd finished speaking he held his thumb up to someone on the other side of the room, who immediately left through the double doors. They'd got me.

After lunch a keynote speaker has to compete with the soporific effects of food and wine. It's usually the sound of applause that wakes people up, rather than any profound insight. It's why we call it the graveyard slot. As I stood up a second time I gripped the familiar lectern and asked myself, "What am I doing here?" My mouth was dry. There was no paper to read. A hushed audience. All I had was a few stories people had told me about why teaching is a noble art. For sixty minutes I'd have little in the way of new evidence, structure or conclusions to draw. Just a few stories.

Aware that I'd stepped in at the last minute, there was generous applause at the end of my presentation. The organisers thanked me profusely. It felt as if I had done just enough to justify their time, realising that compared to the morning with all its hard-edged detail, the afternoon had been what some people would describe as "entertaining".

For the rest of that year, no matter where or when I met colleagues who'd been at that conference, not one of them mentioned my first presentation, which I had so diligently researched and written. On the other hand, time after time people mentioned the stories I told that afternoon. They would tell the story back to me as if I hadn't told it in the first place. The letters and feedback I received kept referring not to the morning as I anticipated but to the afternoon.

The power of stories is that people can see themselves in them. Statistics have their place in seeking clarity, but wisdom comes from another place inside us. It was author John Shea who said that stories begin as a window through which you observe someone else's life. If you listen to the story properly, he says, it ceases to be a window and becomes a mirror. Once that change happens: "You aren't telling the story, the story is telling you." This was the teaching genius of Jesus. He told stories that were so powerful some people heard them and wanted to kill him because of what they saw in the mirror he held up.

There are thirty stories in this book. They are mainly stories of failure rather than heroic success. They speak of my own limitations and my own gradual and reluctant conversion. Nobody likes to learn that they are wrong, especially when it turns out they were wrong about almost everything.

The stories are not aimed at impressing anyone. My hope is that they might connect with your experience and help you to look at things differently. Do not assume that the author is holier than you, cleverer than you, or more deserving than you. The author is a reluctant disciple, who not by his own merit has found himself being taught – not by a course, as good as they can be – but by the simple discovery that if you ask God, he'll start to show you. All you have to do is ask, wait and see.

Chapter 1

The reluctant disciple 1

*As Jesus passed along the Sea of Galilee, he saw
Simon and his brother Andrew casting a net into
the sea – for they were fishermen. And Jesus said
to them, "Follow me and I will make you fish for
people." And immediately they left their nets and
followed him. As he went a little farther, he saw
James son of Zebedee and his brother John, who
were in their boat mending the nets. Immediately
he called them; and they left their father Zebedee
in the boat with the hired men, and followed
him. Jesus went out again beside the sea; the
whole crowd gathered around him, and he taught
them. As he was walking along, he saw Levi son
of Alphaeus sitting at the tax booth, and he said
to him, "Follow me." And he got up and followed
him.*

Mark 1:16-20; 2:13-14

As a small boy I became an altar server. My responsibility
was to assist the priest during church services. This
involved fetching cruets, ringing bells, carrying candles,
looking sad at funerals or joyful at weddings. Most importantly
though, servers were a potential source of new vocations to the
priesthood. For this reason whenever a bishop visited a parish he
would be keen to see many altar servers, a sign of a successful
parish.

In the machinations of my unformed brain, a bishop's visit was
like a state occasion, something akin to a royal event. The

preamble to a bishop's visit involved a lot of very fractious adults double-checking flowers, straightening ties and flicking dandruff from tense shoulders. Everyone was trying to impress upon this visiting dignitary that everything in the community was just as he would want it to be. Brass was polished and windows were cleaned. Everyone was on their best behaviour.

As a boy I had no idea what on earth this was all about. All I knew was that many significant adults in the community were very anxious to impress our visitor. It seemed to me that in order to win his approval it was important that everyone should act properly. All mess, sneezes, creases, stains, noise, improper conduct and any manner of unforeseen incident were to be avoided. Everyone smiled the way they do in photographs, but underlying the smiles was a mixture of corporate pride and extreme anxiety.

The bishop arrived with his secretary, a priest whose task was to train us in the necessary etiquette. As the bishop's assistant he did not put us at our ease. He seemed keen to impress on us the importance of what we were doing, which only made us more afraid. The more precise we needed to be, the greater the potential for error. He told us that after Mass we would line up in the sacristy to meet the bishop. Then he issued this advice, "If the bishop speaks to you answer honestly and succinctly and address him as My Lord."

After Mass we gathered as instructed. We stood aligned, shoulder to shoulder, awaiting what felt like an inspection of the troops. The bishop made his way along the line. He seemed to glide along the corridor as though he was on wheels. He was a tall, slim, imposing man wearing a black cassock and a violet skullcap. I'm sure he never intended to terrify us, but we were picking up our anxieties from the adults around us. As he looked at us I made the fatal mistake of smiling, something I always did when I was nervous. His eye caught mine and his head turned first, then, as if his body was slower to respond, he turned towards me. My heart was racing. "Be honest and succinct, be honest and succinct," I repeated to myself again and again, not knowing what succinct meant.

Leaning forward he smiled and asked me softly, "What do you want to do with the rest of your life?" On reflection I know now that the bishop's concern was for a future supply of priests, but his enquiry was far too abstract for an eight-year-old. It wasn't clear to me what answer he was looking for. Desperate to please and remembering the words of the bishop's secretary "honestly and succinctly", I summoned up the courage to give him the only answer I knew. "Well My Lord," I said, longing to say the right thing, "I want to be a stuntman."

It was easy to gather from the looks of the adults behind him that "stuntman" was in fact the wrong answer. There was one of those brief momentary silences in which everyone looked to the bishop for his response. The correct answer was "priest", but I hadn't seen any films with priests in. The films I watched had explosions in and I wanted to be a stuntman in a James Bond film. "Stuntman," the bishop said, and I saw the emergence of a smile. Looking rather curious he added, "A stuntman, eh? Good lad," and in the blink of an eye he had moved along the line.

Shortly before the end of his tenure as a bishop and more than twenty-five years later he would give me a job in his diocese and I would revisit that story with him. He laughed. He didn't remember the occasion of course, but life had brought us both a long way. "Perhaps you were right," he said. "We are all stuntmen one way or another."

Making connections

At first glance, the response to the call of discipleship looks remarkably straightforward. The New Testament narrative is so rapid it doesn't often give us an insight into the experience of conversion; we see it, but we don't live through it. The calling of

Levi features in three Gospels but the pace of the story gives us little flavour. In Matthew's Gospel he "Got up and followed him", and the same in Mark (2:14). In Luke he "Got up, left everything and followed him" (5:28). Scripture scholars tell me that people like Levi may have known Jesus for some time before they received this calling, yet I'm still perplexed by what happened. What would it be like to be so convinced that you return home and explain, "Look, I haven't got much time. I'm not packing because I've met a compelling man who has changed the way I see things and I need to leave you and go with him. You can have everything." Why would you drop everything, livelihood, family, golf membership and walk into a nomadic and insecure way of life? Was my reluctance both as a child and an adult something to do with the lack of a spectacular religious moment?

A closer inspection of the scriptures gives a more varied response to God's call. Moses, the great leader of the Jewish people, first pleads with God, explaining that he is not a good speaker and requesting that God "send someone else" (Exodus 4:13). Gideon is reluctant and refuses on the basis that he has better brothers. God persists and offers support, so Gideon starts bargaining, asking God to do a miracle. Jonah we read decides to run away from the Lord (Jonah 1:3). Later, when he does relent, we discover the true nature of his reluctance. God has decided not to destroy the people Jonah has been sent to warn and this makes him angry because he feels like a fraud. Isaiah is reluctant because he believes he has a foul mouth. Jeremiah believes himself to be too immature to stand before the people. Ezekiel prostrates himself and has to be repeatedly reassured just to stand up. Zacharias responds to the Angel Gabriel by implying that his message is impossible. The rich young man declines to follow Jesus because of the wealth he has accumulated. Peter calls upon Jesus to leave him because he feels he is too sinful to be a disciple. Thomas is reluctant because he wants evidence. Ananias is reluctant because he fears being arrested. Timothy becomes reluctant because he is overwhelmed by the intellectual ability of the people and struggles to overcome his inadequacy. My favourite example comes from Saul who believes that God has chosen the wrong man! All these responses make the response of Mary the mother of Jesus even more remarkable. Her "yes" is a total surrender to the will of God, even though she will need to ponder these things afterwards.

Not everyone who is called responds with immediate conviction. Not everyone drops everything to follow Jesus the way that Simon, Andrew, James and John do. As a little boy I was not ready to respond to the invitation of the bishop. It was a call I'd have to return to in another guise, many times and much later on in life. For a while I wondered if my lack of desire was unfaithfulness. It wasn't. Saying "yes" to God's call marks the start of a stage in the journey which involves confronting all sorts of reluctances and numerous twists and turns throughout our lives. Reluctance comes in many guises. It is part of the learning, part of the adventure, part of the conversion. Conversion and conviction rarely come in one complete package. Although there are remarkable graced moments along the way, it takes a lifetime to hear and understand our true calling and sometimes we only get to see it looking back.

Conversation starters

- Why are people reluctant to believe in God?
- What helps people to overcome their reluctance?

Chapter 2

Caught sleeping

But about that day or hour no one knows, neither the angels in heaven, nor the Son, but only the Father. Beware, keep alert; for you do not know when the time will come. It is like a man going on a journey, when he leaves home and puts his slaves in charge, each with his work, and commands the doorkeeper to be on the watch. Therefore, keep awake – for you do not know when the master of the house will come, in the evening, or at midnight, or at cockcrow, or at dawn, or else he may find you asleep when he comes suddenly. And what I say to you I say to all: Keep awake.

Mark 13:32-37

When Alison does the shopping she is swift and prudent. She arrives at the shop with a list of the provisions we need in the order in which you come to them in the store. She has plenty of vouchers she has carefully collected from money-off deals. I have remained impressed throughout our marriage at how carefully she prepares herself for everything she does. When I do the shopping a strange mist descends and I get lost in some fluorescent parallel universe. Even though I am provided with a list, I cover twice the distance, circulating around the aisles back and forth. There are items in my trolley I don't remember choosing. I'm easily distracted by products I haven't seen before, such as virgin olive oil with a chilli in the bottle. By the end of the exercise, I have lost my shopping list, spent twice as much on wine as I have on commodities, lost all three children and managed to forget the bread. Supermarkets love people like me. I'm in there for ever.

Three children in a supermarket is a bad idea. As I make my way around the store, Emily sits facing me in the trolley. She is just eighteen months old and she is screaming and screaming for a doughnut. Her mouth is wide open like a small bird clamouring for a worm. The sound is piercing. She draws attention to her long-suffering chauffeur. My determination though is not compromised – I persevere. My older son Sam holds onto the side of the trolley asking questions about why bananas start off green and become yellow, how sausages get their skins, or why women don't have beards. He is six and a half. He walks around the supermarket as though he has hit adolescence early. He stares intently at other shoppers, sullen, sulky and scowling. He wants to go home.

Most worryingly, somewhere else in the shop is Matthew, my middle son, shoplifting a large joint of ham. He is good at it too. He takes all sorts of big shiny things and walks out of the door with them on full view. He never hides what he steals and no one ever stops him. Take your eyes off him for a minute and he's found himself a marrow or non-stick frying pan. Often I'm sitting in the car before I realise what he's taken and have to go back and return it.

There are various responses to this chaos from the other shoppers. Sometimes I get stares of indignation and disapproval. Usually I get sympathy. You can see it in some women's eyes, "Ah bless him," or, "It must be his weekend." Occasionally someone helps me as though I can't reach things. Now and then I get a comment, "She's got good lungs on her," or, "Do you know your son is eating the grapes?"

It was on one such morning when the reaction of a shopper changed my life. When I write that, I don't mean physically. What I encountered in the midst of all this consumer chaos was a prophet and warning of danger from the future. It was the last thing I expected amid a range of grocery promotions.

It is remarkable how many people pass in a supermarket without making eye contact. When my shopping was interrupted I was in my own tiny world examining closely the merits of one pack of bacon over another. As far as I was aware, there was no one around. He was a grey-haired gentleman, nicely appointed, neat and tidy, wearing a shirt and tie for a trip to the supermarket. He had a cheerful disarming disposition as though his lined face was more used to smiling than frowning. Picking up a packet which had fallen from my trolley, he handed it to me and as if oblivious to the disruption Emily was causing, and softly said, "Don't miss it." Somehow, his gentle voice cut through the din of my daughter's screaming: "Growing up," he added, seeing my confusion. More assertively he said again, "Make sure you don't miss them growing up." He clearly felt he needed to reinforce the point.

Although I managed a smile, my interior reaction was not good. His advice did not help me. These were nights of interrupted sleep attending to Emily's painful teething. At 6.30 a.m. that very morning I had been a donkey with a Lego brick in my ear giving rides on my hands and knees. His words irritated me, "What makes you think I'm going to miss them growing up?" I thought. But there was something about him and something about what he said that stayed with me.

We drive up the motorway to a university somewhere up north. Car after car arrives loaded with an assortment of bags, lamps, laptops, cases and boxes. Carrying bundles of these we stumble up a flight of stairs and along a corridor to room five.

"Oh it's not too bad," says Alison as she inspects his new home. "A bit small, but you'll be alright in here," she says, reassuring herself.

We hear laughter in the corridor. "Go and meet your new neighbours," we say to Sam. He leaves the room to embrace his new life.

Alison begins to unpack, neatly folding the clothes she has ironed and laying them carefully into the top draw. She places a toothbrush in a glass by the sink.

"I think it's time we went," I say. She agrees. There isn't much to say. It's time for us to go. Seeing her pain I say to her, "I love you." She looks at me sharply and says, "Don't go there!"

It is difficult to imagine a situation in which telling your wife you love her will get you into trouble. This is one of those moments. She is holding it all together.

He came back to me. That man in the supermarket. As we drove home without our boy, that man came back to me. Eighteen years of parenting had passed by so quickly. It wasn't advice he had given to me all those years ago, it was a confession.

👥 Making connections

Seeing me in all my chaos surrounded by sticky fingers, confusion and a screaming child, the man in the supermarket realised he'd missed it. He'd missed what mattered in his life. It isn't that hard to do. For all sorts of good reasons, we devote our lives to all sorts of distractions, only to wonder later on if we have somehow missed out. This is why grandchildren provide so many people with healing.

The scriptures have a lot to say about time: understanding it, reading it, attributing it. In Mark's Gospel there is a warning about being alert to the end of time. The early Church took it literally and began to prepare for the second coming of Christ. Yet it isn't the threat of the end days which matters here. What matters is not to sleep walk through our lives. It isn't fearing death so much as fearing a life never lived. Several stories in the Gospels speak of being ready, alert, awake and sensitive to what is happening. This is a mystical alertness. It is not nostalgia. Something is dying and something is emerging all through our lives. Being awake to that makes us appreciative and grateful. It helps us to prepare ourselves for a life lived to the full and it helps us to accept change when it comes, even when the change incorporates loss. The alternative is that like the man in the supermarket we become wistful, grieving the life we didn't have.

Catholics used to carry something called *A Penny Catechism* – a short book of questions and answers to live by. As they went to bed, it encouraged them to prepare for death. What initially sounds morbid was actually meant to teach people how to live. If we live our lives as though each day may be our last, we greet each new dawn with delight. Each day becomes a gift and a chance to get it right. Alternatively we can live for the weekend, our next holiday or our pension. One day we see a young version of us and, without realising it, we speak to our younger self: "Don't miss them growing up," we say.

Conversation starters

- Is it possible to sleep walk through our lives?
- What causes us to lose sight of what is important?

Chapter 3

Hardened hearts

*When evening came, the boat was out on the sea,
and he was alone on the land. When he saw that
they were straining at the oars against an adverse
wind, he came towards them early in the morning,
walking on the sea. He intended to pass them by.
But when they saw him walking on the sea, they
thought it was a ghost and cried out; for they all
saw him and were terrified. But immediately he
spoke to them and said, "Take heart, it is I; do
not be afraid." Then he got into the boat with
them and the wind ceased. And they were utterly
astounded, for they did not understand about the
loaves, but their hearts were hardened.*

Mark 6:47-52

Long before Ofsted was conceived of and performance became the purpose of it all, there was a time in teaching when the staff room was a safe haven. During my first years in teaching I lived on adrenalin and hard work, but there was normally a brief reprieve during the lunch hour when I could retreat briefly back into an adult world.

In most staff rooms there would be a photocopier, a sink full of dirty mugs, a macabre sculpture of a skull with a nail in it, a tea urn, a stack of pigeonholes stuffed with paperwork, a video recorder with a cassette of *Chariots of Fire* stuck in it, and a table in the corner with an overhead projector sitting on it. Big boxy computers had arrived but no pupil possessed a mobile phone and the internet was not there to provide all the answers. The old-fashioned pastoral deputy, an endangered species, had a dartboard on the wall of his office and a small handful of teachers still went to the pub on a Friday lunchtime.

These were also the last years when the staff room in many schools resembled something of a television sitcom. You would find a variety of characters. There would be the staff room clown who would come in wearing the knife-through-the-head hat he'd just confiscated. There would be the unconventional and slightly alternative English teacher with a penchant for dyeing her hair and street theatre. Three grumpy long-suffering servants would sit in the corner, grimacing at any new idea and mumbling, "I remember the last time they thought up this one," before adding "… and it didn't work then." There would be the supremely efficient but slightly officious PA to the head teacher who made you feel disorganised. There would be a school caretaker who would take you to one side for a good swear, and a young PE teacher who all the teenagers fancied. Most obvious of all was the newly qualified teacher carrying a huge pile of books under one arm, a rolled-up poster under another, a set of keys gripped in their teeth, a carrier bag full of text books and the look of distress written across their forehead. In 1985 that was me, along with Kate, and we were both aiming to survive as much as succeed. Get to July without breaking down in your appraisal, and you've made it.

Under the intense pressure of our difficult first year, my fellow fresher Kate was about to break every convention of the staff room, spectacularly! The usual things were going on. The moaners had gathered in the corner for their daily huddle, the Tupperware teachers were picking their way through couscous and coriander, the "lads" had gathered by the tea urn to talk sport, and the deputy head was having an impromptu meeting with a supply teacher about her version of events in an "incident" that morning. It was pretty standard procedure.

Kate bounded into the staff room. Almost hyperventilating, she announced, "I've just taught year nine. It was bloody fantastic!" Teaching year nine was everyone's job. It hardly merited a round of applause.

Anxious to justify herself, she continued, "I hate year nine, I really do," before listing the notorious pupils she had the misfortune to teach.

Then, still breathless, she explained: "I tried turning it all into a quiz, with prizes, and I was sure they'd laugh at it, but they started to go for it, and then the lads on the back row joined in and one by one they were putting their hand up to answer my questions and, and… when the lesson ended they came up to me and said 'Miss, can we do that again tomorrow?'"

After her frantic account she stood there, unsure what to do next. The staff room fell silent. A collective "What?" and a sense of confusion hung in the room until, one by one, people returned to their conversations. It was as if someone had broken an important rule, but no one quite knew what it was.

I was in the corner next to the tea urn, standing next to a more experienced teacher. He looked at me, lifted his mug in the direction of Kate, and said, "What was that about?"

"Good on her," I said. After all, I knew personally what her struggle felt like. It was my struggle too.

He, though, had been teaching for quite some time. "You see that," he raised his mug again, "I used to be like that," and then laughed as if I should too.

Looking at him, I found myself wondering whether, if I had kids, I would prefer them to have Kate's zeal and enthusiasm, or his seasoned experience?

It was a strange moment. I could see people's mouths moving but although I was going along with it I couldn't hear them; I wasn't listening. I noticed Kate, now sitting with a colleague and chatting, still about her lesson. She had discovered that she could reach the difficult ones. We should have opened the champagne.

Suddenly it dawned on me what rule Kate had broken. Somewhere someone had decided that cynicism was more intelligent than joy. When did that happen? When did we decide that enthusiasm is naïve? It turns out that it isn't just our arteries that can harden as we get older, but our hearts also. The real tragedy when our hearts become hardened, as with our circulation, is that we don't realise it's happening until it's too late.

👥 Making connections

The general response of people in the Bible upon coming into the presence of almightiness is incredibly underwhelming. In the passage from Mark's Gospel we meet a group of disciples who don't understand what they are encountering. Having witnessed Jesus feeding a multitude with meagre resources you'd think they would be impressed and excited. They are not. We read that they have "hardened" their hearts.

It is not a new problem. After their daring escape from Egypt across the Red Sea, the people quickly have enough of the desert; thirsty and tired at Marah and Rephidim, they threaten Moses and complain to God. They begin to prefer their old captivity and moan about their freedom. When the Apostle Paul is writing to the Hebrews he warns them not to harden their hearts as they did against Moses in the desert. It seems that a truly mystical encounter has a remarkably temporary impact. The theme of a hardened heart returns regularly through the scriptures. It is as if we begin life open to receive and gradually close down.

The problem with a hardened heart is that it replaces a grateful disposition with a complaining one. We lose our sense of gladness and we become moaners. We stop being excited by life, surprised by things, enthusiastic; we laugh less, we don't vote or try to improve things, we stop learning, we stop going to meetings and, worst of all, we don't tell her that we love her any more because she already knows. We can lose our love for life itself without really noticing.

Once, when I was queuing at Heathrow to check in for my long-haul flight, I was told that my flight had been cancelled. I'd be delayed for a day because the pilot had had a heart attack. I'd be stuck in a local hotel and lose a day from my trip. I was immediately aware that the small print in my insurance would not cover this. Looking at the logo of the huge international company, I complained to the check-in assistant, "But you are a big company," I said. "You must have more than one pilot." The lady in the queue behind me leant forward, and said pointedly within my hearing, "I'm sorry to hear about the pilot, I hope he recovers." Oh dear! What is happening to me?

So whose words flow out of my mouth, the newly qualified teacher who dreams of making a difference, or the weary cynic who lives in the "real world"? Be careful what you say at check-in. "O that today you would listen to his voice! Do not harden your hearts" (Psalm 95:7-8).

Conversation starters

- Has life taught us to be more enthusiastic or cynical?
- How do we stop ourselves from developing hardened hearts?

Chapter 4

Killing off your friends

Then they came to Capernaum; and when he was in the house he asked them, "What were you arguing about on the way?" But they were silent, for on the way they had argued with one another who was the greatest. He sat down, called the twelve, and said to them, "Whoever wants to be first must be last of all and servant of all." Then he took a little child and put it among them; and taking it in his arms, he said to them, "Whoever welcomes one such child in my name welcomes me, and whoever welcomes me welcomes not me but the one who sent me."

Mark 9:33-37

In her mid-fifties my mum suffered an extreme heart attack. During the by-pass surgery which saved her, the team of surgeons, doctors and nurses had to break her ribs, transfer her functioning heart onto a bed of ice to slow it down and, taking veins from her legs, provide new arteries around blocked ones. The remarkable surgery included replacing her entire blood and lasted almost a day. The effect of the anaesthetic took many days to wear off. The entire procedure was a remarkable feat of medical skill in what would have been considered an impossible procedure only a generation before.

Three days later my mum is learning to walk again. When we visit her in the hospital ward we find her taking tiny steps away from her bed. Like a child, she is concentrating on every move, grimacing occasionally when she pushes herself too hard. She holds onto the saline pole which follows her on wheels. "It's not my time yet," she says repeatedly, as though she were defying death itself. She is learning to move again so that she may ultimately walk back into her life. She is already feisty and determined. "I'm going to see your kids grow up," she insists, and commits to another step.

I realised through my mum's experience the power of the camaraderie that people feel when they face terrible ordeals together. Recovery can be a slow process and loving visitors can only sympathise from the sidelines. There was good humour in that ward, and the staff and patients obviously knew how to keep each other going. Although there are lots of people around, a hospital can be a lonely place, and it's often other patients, facing the same challenges, who provide each other with wisdom, understanding, life stories, and the kind of mutual support they really need.

Determined to exercise again, my mum took another exhausting trip from the bed to the window – a journey which took her past six other beds. As she stepped towards the brightness of the window, she met a man moving towards her at the same pace, wearing the same scars, pulling the same pole and drip. Having come so close to death you would imagine that two people who have suffered the same violent surgery might share a greater understanding and wisdom.

As they met my mum said, "Hello."

The man didn't introduce himself but instead asked: "Did you have a double or a triple?"

He was enquiring about the number of by-passes my mum had had.

"A double," she replied.

As if to reassure himself, he said, "Ah, I had a triple."

Pointing over her shoulder, he added, "That's Arthur over there, he's new."

"Oh yes," said my mum, "I saw him come in yesterday."

Holding up four fingers as if he needed to illustrate the point, he said, "Quadruple!"

It seemed there was some sort of contest going on, and Arthur had clearly won.

"Well done to Arthur," my mum said, and continued her quest for the light and the view from the window.

This strange conversation led me to wonder. What was the first thing I ever compared myself with? When I ask that question to teachers who work with small children they usually answer "age". Children declare their age in almost the first conversation they have: "I'm four," they say, in order to establish seniority. At that age, there is no need to justify or qualify this kind of statement. The reply might be, "I'm four and a quarter." Job done. Ranking established. From there the conversation moves quickly to stuff. Children boast about their possessions in a way that adults would love to, but can't. If you have the latest computer game, phone or football boots you are going to tell people as often as you can. Whatever is new relegates older stuff with instant effect. Only the most personal possessions survive, the rest are obsolete.

For teenagers the boast is about friends and partners. Teenagers often define their self-worth by how others view them. When a teenager gets a valentine card she immediately tells everyone. For the same reason, teenage courting rituals include public displays of affection. Teens also compulsively monitor performance – their own and each other's. If you're lucky enough to pass the tests that adults set you – exams, driving tests, awards or interviews – you want it announced in the local paper so that your peers know what you've achieved. Of course it's no bad thing, if a little embarrassing, to celebrate success.

Once we're on our career paths, we learn to advertise our success through symbols of wealth. Although it is culturally unacceptable to declare what we earn, we may buy a personalised numberplate, or make sure we have the right labels on our clothes. It is not wrong to want these things, but having got them we often can't help but advertise the fact in some subtle way. At this point a sub-group forms, of people who boast about the size of their overdrafts or their lack of wealth. This "inverse snobbery" is an alternative way of declaring our self-worth by suggesting non-conformism, but at its root we are still comparing ourselves with other people.

As our careers take off we climb to positions of authority which bring us further signs of self-worth. These might include letters after our name, a more important job title, a bigger office, a higher place in the boardroom. Wanting authority in order to change things is again a good thing, but the status which comes with it is a reward we can't help but display, or indeed envy when we see it in others. It is not uncommon to hear someone ask, "I wonder what they're worth," referring only to someone's financial status.

Around mid-life, those of us lucky enough to have a family start to boast about our children. If Sally passes her oboe exam, it must go in the Christmas card. Joe's final call-up for the school team is also duly noted in the typed "round robin" letter we fold into the card. By return, we read about our nieces' and nephews' successes and accomplishments.

One winter's evening, in a city parish near the heart of Plymouth, we were running a session we called "Cash in the Attic". It was aimed at those we politely referred to in the publicity as being "in the autumn of their lives". These lovely people in their seventies and eighties had gathered to see what wisdom there might be from the Church about ageing, retirement, death and grief. Despite the apparently morbid theme there was plenty of laughter and a lot of wine. We are often so busy caught up in technology and considering the future that we forget that church communities have a strong appeal to those for whom death is a clear and present danger. There is nothing quite like death to focus our questions about eternity.

At one of these sessions I took the liberty of asking: "Can anybody tell me please, what those who reach their eighties boast about?" It seemed that I'd seen the great boasts of childhood, teenage years and adulthood; I too had compared my house, my car, my children, my entire life to other people's. How, though, would a person in their eighties compare themselves to their peers? A spritely elderly gentleman in the centre of the room raised his hand. After all these years, I thought, the things we were taught to do at school stay with us. Having caught my attention with his raised hand, he waited for silence before saying: "All my friends are dead!" There was laughter and I was speechless. How do you respond to a statement like that? He had outlived his friends and in doing so he had won. So I said, "Well done," and he got a round of applause, because his friends are dead and he isn't.

As I drove home I realised that he had said something important. It became apparent that whenever there is news of a sudden death nationally in the local news, the first question that comes to people's minds is, "How old were they?" The question isn't what really matters for the deceased or their families. Knowing someone's age doesn't really change anything. The question might be evidence of a more egotistical curiosity. How am I doing compared to the deceased? It may be that even the length of our lives becomes a contest.

What is the last thing we ever boast about? In speaking to some care assistants in a local nursing home, it turns out that it may finish exactly where it starts. Just as we did as children, in an old people's home we might greet our fellow residents with our new-found status, "I'm ninety-four, you know." As T. S. Eliot wrote:

> What we call the beginning is often the end
> And to make an end is to make a beginning.
> The end is where we start from.

▲ Making connections

Imagine witnessing the biggest popular movement in Palestine for centuries and becoming part of it. Crowds are pressing upon you for access to Jesus. Inside the movement, however, there is quiet discord. Who will Jesus award his key positions to? Who will he appoint to sit nearest to him? You become aware of everything you gave up to follow him. Surely you are worthy of recognition? The various talents and abilities of the others make you feel insecure. Colleagues and peers become a threat to your position. Unconsciously you are arguing about who is the greatest, without realising how sad that is.

Our culture defines our success by our ranking. Everything measureable becomes a league table. Imagine devoting a lifetime to measuring your worth by comparing yourself to others. What a disaster that would be for our confidence and maturity. We were able to find joy in most things before we began to compare ourselves to the others.

Jesus is aware of the way in which our insecurity feeds our need to make comparisons: "This is not to happen among you," he insists. In John's Gospel we find Jesus washing the dirt off his followers' feet in order to drive home the point. He will insist that his followers have the courage to let their feet be washed and the humility to wash the feet of others. Both washing and being washed mean that we abandon our need to win. The alternative is a lifetime comparing, losing confidence and being resentful on the one hand or relegating others as lesser than ourselves on the other.

Competition works well in sport, but as a way of living it is ultimately empty. It is important to strive, to persist, to endeavour, to try and keep trying. But once our life becomes a comparison we will fall into envy or insecurity. We will start to argue. To outlive our friends was never an achievement. It was a gift. Along with everything else. To see it any other way is the beginning of our downfall.

Conversation starters

- Is it a good thing to compare ourselves to others?
- Does the achievement of others cause you delight or envy?

Chapter 5

They'll never replace me

*He told them this parable: "Which one of you,
having a hundred sheep and losing one of them,
does not leave the ninety-nine in the wilderness
and go after the one that is lost until he finds it?
When he has found it, he lays it on his shoulders
and rejoices. And when he comes home, he calls
together his friends and neighbours, saying to
them, 'Rejoice with me, for I have found my sheep
that was lost.' Just so, I tell you, there will be more
joy in heaven over one sinner who repents than
over ninety-nine righteous persons who need no
repentance."*

Luke 15:3-7

I'm not sure why restlessness surfaces but sometimes in life, even when things are going well, it is time to move on. My time in the school had come to an end even though it had been the happiest possible start to a career. Because I had moved to the area for the job, the friends I had made were connected to the school. Ilkeston, a tight mining community in the East Midlands, had quickly become home to me. In that dirty old town, I was a happy young man.

It was not possible to escape the job there. Buying wine in a local supermarket, the girl at the checkout would be fishing for gossip: "Are you having someone special round for dinner, sir?" She would be in school on Monday telling everyone I have a girlfriend. The receptionist at the surgery, the parent of a pupil in year eight, would greet me with, "Good morning, Mr Wells". Even the doorman outside the pub on Bath Street was a past pupil who would say, "Evening, Mr Wells, anyone gives you any trouble come and get me."

One of the reasons the school was a happy place was that the teachers who had worked there for many years were cheerful people who enjoyed what they did. It created a certain stability which was a good platform on which to learn your profession. The camaraderie only made the decision to leave all the more painful. To help justify the decision, I would console myself with egotistical thoughts of how hard I had worked and how difficult it would be for them to find someone to replace me. In my youthful conceit I imagined that I would leave a hole they couldn't fill. How could they? As a young man without a family I lived for my job, arriving early each day and leaving late, with few distractions beyond the social dimension of the school. How could they replace that kind of dedication?

On the last day of term the pupils were sent home at lunchtime and, once we had packed them off on the school buses, there would be a party for the staff and a huge collective sigh of relief. Always a happy occasion, the staff party was a chance to say goodbye to leavers. This time it was my turn. Kind cards, the promise of keeping in touch and a few gifts made leaving all the harder. In lovely summer sunshine with a glass of Pinot Grigio, I began to doubt my decision. "Why would you leave this?" I thought, but I reassured myself that at least "they'll never replace me".

They replaced me with consummate ease. By September that year, another committed teacher was proving himself in my old job, and the school not only replaced me, but flourished without me. For all that I gave that place, it had given me more, and the community had filled the hole I had left by morning break of day one. To this day I remain grateful to the staff and I would never wish them ill, but my pride got the better of me, and I regretted that, given how much sweat I had exerted there, the school didn't just briefly – for a day or two at least – fall completely to pieces in my absence.

As the staff drifted home and the promise of an evening in the pub beckoned, I took myself away from the party and wandered the corridors for the last time. I was remembering my first day in the place and how scared I had been. Every classroom, corridor and office had a story to tell. It was all recorded in the bricks and mortar. It didn't take long to remove my personal effects from my office, leave my keys on the secretary's desk and empty my mailbox in the staff room. In the staff room there was a real haunting – everyone had gone but I could hear all their voices. I was starting to get sentimental. It was time to walk into the next chapter of my life, so standing before a room of empty chairs I whispered, "Thank you." The voice of an unseen caretaker behind me said politely, "You're welcome."

It was late afternoon and I was walking to the staff car park. The box I was carrying contained a few books, a framed photograph from my desk, farewell cards and a few bottles of wine I'd been given. It was an effort fumbling for my car keys while balancing the box against the side of the car. Holding the door open with my knee I became aware of someone standing behind me, a reflection in the car window.

Martin was standing there awkwardly, like teenagers do. His arms looked too long for his body. His uniform had always been too big for him, but recently he'd grown rapidly and now his blazer extended not far beyond his elbows. He'd got ink on his collar and a plaster on his earlobe covering a failed attempt to pierce his ear with a metal compass. Martin was one of the boys I had spent a lot of time with, especially around the time his mum and dad separated. He was likeable, yet he just wasn't really suited to school life. Like his uniform, he didn't quite fit. Some teachers used to really shout at him, but it never seemed to bother him much.

"Martin?" I said. It sounded like a question. "Martin, what happened, did you miss your bus?" It wasn't especially unusual to see him walking home after missing his bus. He lived near me, so sometimes, in an age when it wasn't considered unprofessional, I'd offer him a lift home. He didn't say anything, which wasn't like him. "Get in," I said, "I'll take you home." It was now two hours since the buses had left. "Sir," he said, almost standing to attention and ignoring my offer. "Sir," he repeated, as if about to make a speech to the House of Commons, "I just wanted to say that you was alright!"

What a fool am I? They can replace my name on an office door with a screwdriver. As for Martin, they'll never replace me.

Making connections

In John's Gospel, the High Priest Caiaphas advocates losing one man (Jesus) for the sake of the people. In this parable, Jesus appears to suggest that we risk losing the people for the sake of one man (sheep). What kind of success would come from devoting all your energy to one per cent of your responsibilities? Why would Jesus encourage such a disproportionate investment? Couldn't you do more good if you concentrated on the greatest good for the greatest number? Doesn't that make better leadership sense and lead to more rejoicing?

When we devote all our energy to improving systems or raising standards we can make efficiencies but there is a risk. No one sets out to do this intentionally, but as leaders in health provision we can forget patients, as leaders in education we can forget children, even in church communities we can lose sight of people. Jesus doesn't ask his followers to resolve the problem of poverty, just as he doesn't ask them to remove a vicious brutal occupying army. At times he appears almost disinterested in using administrative, political, ecclesial or strategic thinking. He focuses his followers' attention on the individuals they meet. He knows that the integrity of the people who follow him will arise out of these personal encounters. It is the small everyday things we do that will ultimately be the fertile soil of our success and the source of our joy.

The boy had been waiting for me, his speech rehearsed: "You was alright." These words help me to understand why we are all in the end, irreplaceable. It isn't the school's improvement plan or raised performance that will be held in the memory and affection of others. What lasts is sketched inside relationships. What becomes eternal is the simple impact we have on one another's lives. Martin was the reason I made a difference and no school improvement plan would have recorded it the way he did. The school didn't need me. Martin did. His life and mine, his time and mine, entwined briefly. That should be enough. The rest was my ego.

Conversation starters

- How do we measure success?
- Are there better ways to measure a life?

Chapter 6

Giving 'til it hurts

He sat down opposite the treasury, and watched the crowd putting money into the treasury. Many rich people put in large sums. A poor widow came and put in two small copper coins, which are worth a penny. Then he called his disciples and said to them, "Truly I tell you, this poor widow has put in more than all those who are contributing to the treasury. For all of them have contributed out of their abundance; but she out of her poverty has put in everything she had, all she had to live on."

Mark 12:41-44

In the Plateau state of northern Nigeria is the city of Jos – a vibrant lively place, filled with half a million people all travelling at the same time in every direction on noisy motorbikes. These small bikes are used with spectacular ingenuity to carry carpets, dogs and melons, with someone somewhere underneath steering. Occasionally you'll see a whole family piled onto one. Several times I saw five people on a single motorbike. Health and safety regulations seem barely to exist here, nor do helmets, road signs, or road markings. There are traffic signals, but no one seems to heed them. Yet everyone seems to get where they need to. There is commerce of course, traders on every street corner selling fruit, trousers, motorbike tyres or sunglasses. Inside all this dusty chaos are pockets of wealth, immense poverty and violent religious tensions. It is a boisterous, colourful, troubled city, choked by motorbike fumes.

As a visitor I am taking part in an orientation organised by CAFOD, a leading charity in the area. Through them I will see how donations are distributed and how projects are run. My motive is to become an ambassador for the sorts of projects CAFOD are doing there.

Firstly we visit an orphanage supported by donations. We meet the first victims of poverty, children. They are cared for by loving staff and are clean, well fed and safe, although they seem unusually serious for small children. They are pleased to see us, but they are intent on examining our appearance, more curious than playful.

Our second visit is to a hospital, a sparse facility by Western standards, with very little in the way of medical technology. The hospital is clean and well organised, but the wards are furnished with only beds and tables. There are no scanners, no beeping heart monitors. There is that strange mixture of tragedy and joy which is hard to describe without sounding patronising. I'm struck by the dedication and cheerfulness of the staff and by the acceptance of suffering among the patients. Despite so little in the way of resources, no one is complaining or thumping the desk. No one is shouting at some bewildered receptionist. It is hard not to be ashamed of how rarely I feel wealthy and how quickly I am prepared to complain if I have to wait a while in accident and emergency. Yet here in Jos, walking through these wards, I am a rich man and I know it.

It is lunchtime and we are given a small loaf and a bottle of water. The sun vertically above us beats down and for a moment I take delight in the intense heat. There are no shadows. This is not really a good time to be outside, but I will enjoy the bright heat for a while. On the parched street outside I am alone for the first time in the day. A bench outside the entrance provides me with a brief opportunity to relax and reflect upon the morning.

My thoughts are about what I am learning, not just about the good work I see, or the importance of giving, but about how right it is to be here. To experience this place is broadening my horizon, widening my perspective, challenging my insular world view, making me a better person. It is not difficult among these thoughts to begin to feel good about myself. When I get back I will think about how I can support this charity and I determine to make a difference. Before I embarked upon this trip my intention was to be challenged and as I think about the orphanage and hospital I know that I will go home a different person.

Tearing at the paper bag which contains my bread and lifting it to my mouth, my attention is distracted by a small boy. My meal is interrupted. It is clear that I am not alone and in the company of a patient child. He stands close to me, staring with huge brown eyes. Looking intently, his face expressionless, he is not asking. With humility and hope, he is waiting for my generosity.

For a brief moment I am aware of my own hunger. For a moment I think of the importance of what I am doing here and how it is important that I eat. Yet I know what to do. This boy standing in my space, intruding on my lunch break, needs this more than I do. Taking each end of the bread roll I break it into two equal pieces. Leaning forward I barely hold it out before he reaches out to receive it. Taking his portion from me carefully, but not snatching it, he runs away across the road in front of the hospital, over a low brick wall and into a dirty compound.

Alone again, I'm feeling slightly deprived that he didn't want to talk. I'm slightly disappointed that my little offering didn't buy a smile or start a conversation. When the children here smile it is impossible not to be affected by their joy. "He was in a hurry to eat, he must have been very hungry," I think, and I content myself in the knowledge that I have done the right thing. I'd have liked to sit here with him, eating together. Never mind. He will enjoy his half and I will enjoy mine.

My focus is back on my bread. As I start to eat it, I'm distracted by a commotion taking place over the road. In the dust and haze of the midday heat I make out several children in a huddle, noisily enjoying the other half of my loaf as it is broken into small pieces and distributed by that small boy among his friends.

Making connections

There is something a bit annoying about sympathy. Many of us don't really take to the idea of people feeling sorry for us. Disabled people can often find sympathy offensive rather than helpful. Sympathy comes from a Greek word which means "fellow feeling". To be offered sympathy is kind but it doesn't really do much for us in practical terms. Compassion on the other hand comes from a Latin word *compassio,* the root of which means "to suffer with". Compassion involves a willingness to share pain. Sympathy and compassion are often confused but they are profoundly different. Compassion includes a practical dimension. In his 2014 Lenten address Pope Francis put it like this: "Let us not forget that real poverty hurts. No self-denial is real without this dimension of penance. I distrust charity that costs nothing and does not hurt."

In Mark's Gospel we find Jesus sitting opposite the treasury observing a variety of people, each of them giving the common offering for the poor. He sits far enough away not to be noticed. It is fascinating to imagine him people-watching this way. He uses the generosity of a vulnerable widow to teach his disciples a radical lesson. Through her two coins he teaches them that she is giving more than all those who are giving from what they have left over. Our giving should not be measured by its monetary worth, but by what it demands of us. She gives not from a place of sympathy but from compassion. The widow gives more, since through her sacrifice she will share the pain of others. Jesus challenges the idea that charity is about achieving great sums or beating last year's total. What we give should cause us to take on in some quiet way the pain of another. In this way, much of what we mean by "true love" is often compassion, "for better for worse" is to be shared.

As I sat on that bench outside the hospital I was being taught a tough lesson by a small boy with half a bread roll. There I was feeling satisfied that I had shared what I had, but the boy's giving shed a new perspective on my own. My offering was sympathetic. My hunger would still be satisfied by what I held back. There was no true sacrifice. His situation and mine would remain unaltered. Yet taught by that little lad, all I could think was, "David Wells, you have got a lot to learn." It was important to me that I would be challenged by this trip. What really surprised me was that the challenge came not from a future resolution or some disturbing and insurmountable problem to be resolved, but from what I already had in my hand. The bread in my hand was evidence that I had yet to be as mighty as a widow with two coins, or a small boy in a dusty compound.

Conversation starters

- When do we feel a sense of our own privilege?
- When do we notice in ourselves a sense of compassion?

Chapter 7

"'Proper' but loveless"

When the Pharisees heard that he had silenced the Sadducees, they gathered together, and one of them, a lawyer, asked him a question to test him. "Teacher, which commandment in the law is the greatest?" He said to him, "'You shall love the Lord your God with all your heart, and with all your soul, and with all your mind.' This is the greatest and first commandment. And a second is like it: 'You shall love your neighbour as yourself.' On these two commandments hang all the law and the prophets."

Matthew 22:34-40

Like so many young boys, my sons wanted to be super-heroes. They role played among the stars in a distant universe or on the deck of a pirate ship. At bedtime they'd ask me for war stories and testimonies of courage and daring. Winning or losing in these stories was not the issue, it was the fight against evil that captured their spirit. In their teens, Hollywood became the great storyteller, filling their imaginations with spectacular images of heroism and explosions.

In his formative years one such movie, *Saving Private Ryan*, captured the imagination of my eldest son. In the opening scene we see a cemetery in Normandy and watch an elderly man with his family standing at the graveside of the soldier who had saved his life. Through his eyes we are taken back in time to the carnage of 6 June 1944, and the story of this particular relationship becomes the substance of the movie.

While holidaying one summer in northern France, we were inspired by movies like *Saving Private Ryan* to visit the Normandy beaches where men had spilt real blood. My sons' own great-uncle had disembarked from a landing craft in 1944 and, despite surviving the war, had spoken little of his own ordeal. Visiting the beaches we could step at least in part into his story. In contrast to the war games of their imagination, I wanted the boys to begin to sense what being a hero might really feel like.

A visit to a historically significant place can open your senses to something you can never gain from a history lesson or a movie. Whether standing in the memorial to the victims of 9/11, a trench on the Somme, or stepping into the harrowing site of the bomb blast in Hiroshima, the past lingers like a long shadow. It leaves its mark.

It is not possible to truly grasp the sacrifice, heroism and sheer stupidity of war until you stand among an expanse of white crosses in a war cemetery. The cemetery at Colleville is situated on a high green plateau overlooking what was codenamed Omaha Beach. There, 9,386 graves stand in perfect alignment, each facing towards the homeland of he who lies beneath. I have visited many such cemeteries, but few are as large or as overwhelming. The manicured shrubs and neatly cut grass give the impression of a place of serenity and pristine beauty, but the tragic significance of each grave draws you back into the terrible chaos that once was here. We visit on a sunny day and behind the graves there is a perfect view of swathes of golden sand and a blue ocean. For such a relatively small stretch of sand, and the rocky path leading up to this place, nine thousand men fell to the ground in a hail of bullets. Historians tell us that Omaha Beach was a catastrophe, a military nightmare, where the sea itself became blood red from the sheer number of casualties.

Standing before such a scene, you can't help but fall silent and contemplate. The boys grasped it all in a second; many heroes don't come home. There was no need to labour the point. They recognised the courage and sacrifice on the one hand, and the tragic wastefulness on the other. These things would continue to impress upon us all, long after the visit.

Lost in awe at the scene, I had failed to notice two beautiful little girls running through the rows of white crosses completely unaware of the solemnity that had descended upon the three of us. These girls were having a wonderful time picking flowers from the borders and throwing them first on one grave and then on another. Their arms outstretched like aircraft, they swooped and cavorted, their long blond hair catching the wind as they ran.

The schoolteacher in me came to the fore. Their behaviour was not right for this context. The girls had to be respectful and someone had to parent them. It seemed only right that it should be me, especially as one of them was my daughter!

I called the girls and they skipped through the lanes of graves towards me, beaming with innocence and joy. It was sunny after all, and Emily was wearing her yellow dress. Just wearing it made her happy. She was seven years old. Moving quickly towards them I gathered their childish energy into my arms. On my knees with my arms outstretched I said, "Girls, this place is... unusual, I think we should be quiet here. Let's play your game on the beach this afternoon." Looking around I pointed out the other people in the cemetery, and suggested that they might not appreciate the game they were playing. This all sounded quite reasonable to me. I was being responsible. The girls' arms fell to their sides. My anxiety was fed by how I imagined the other visitors were feeling. Conscious of others, I wanted to turn down the volume and enthusiasm of this tender pair.

One such visitor was a very tall, elderly gentleman, a serious-looking man with a chest full of medals and an American accent.

These medals alerted me to the fact that his connection with this place was closer than mine. I didn't dare ask, but I sensed he had seen this place in all its devastation. He deserved peace and quiet. He saw my parenting and slowly made his way towards us. Standing up to greet him, he looked at me reproachfully and with simple dignity whispered, "Leave the girls alone." Seeing on my face a look of surprise, he added, "Why do you think the guys died?"

He walked past me, patting my shoulder once, as if he recognised what he'd just done. The last thing I expected was to be chastised. A prophet always sneaks upon you when you least expect one. Ashamed, I thought of the times I have stood policing religious occasions, shushing and glaring, as if that was what God wanted: regulation rather than joy. The sacrifice in this bloodied field was for a purpose, for joy, not misery, for yellow dresses not black ones. There was more life in that little girl's yellow dress than in all my religious indignation and something more worth dying for.

Making connections

Life is filled with regulation. Regulations keep us safe, they keep order and help us to organise ourselves. Wherever we collaborate, people look for clarity of roles, definition of purpose, contracts and agreements. Laws serve all these purposes. In Matthew's Gospel, the Pharisee calls upon Jesus to identify which of all the laws is the greatest. Scripture scholars tell us that at the time of Jesus the law was made up of at least six hundred regulations based upon the Ten Commandments.

Jesus draws together the love of God and love of neighbour as the essence of all law. In choosing two answers rather than one, he unites them. Pope Benedict XVI writes, "Love of God and love of neighbour are thus inseparable. They form a single commandment" *(Deus Caritas Est, 18)*.

When the love of God and the love of neighbour are separated, they can produce strange religious behaviour. Worshipping God becomes an obligation, lacking in love, while serving our neighbour becomes a duty, lacking sincere compassion. Pope Benedict beautifully expresses this when he teaches:

> If I have no contact whatsoever with God in my life, then I cannot see in the other anything more than the other, and I am incapable of seeing in him the image of God. But if in my life I fail completely to heed others, solely out of a desire to be devout and to perform my "religious duties", then my relationship with God will also grow arid. It becomes merely "proper", but loveless.
>
> *Deus Caritas Est*, 18

Standing in that cemetery I understood my own tendency to supplant love with regulation. The elderly prophet was able to encompass both solemnity and joy without undermining either, because he loved the men he was honouring. Sadly, it does seem possible to live a life properly and yet without love. Our faith, our work and even our marriages can so easily become proper but loveless. We are at risk of this whenever we do religion without love for each other and whenever we try to love each other without God's help. This state of affairs is described by Jesus when he laments, "This people honours me with their lips, but their hearts are far from me" (Matthew 15:8). In my effort to teach my daughter something laudable and right, I forgot the yellow dress.

Conversation starters

- Is our effort to be thorough ever at the expense of something else?
- What does it mean to act properly but without love?

Chapter 8

Laying down our weapons

Then Pilate entered the headquarters again, summoned Jesus, and asked him, "Are you the King of the Jews?" Jesus answered, "Do you ask this on your own, or did others tell you about me?" Pilate replied, "I am not a Jew, am I? Your own nation and the chief priests have handed you over to me. What have you done?" Jesus answered, "My kingdom is not from this world. If my kingdom were from this world, my followers would be fighting to keep me from being handed over to the Jews. But as it is, my kingdom is not from here." Pilate asked him, "So you are a king?" Jesus answered, "You say that I am a king. For this I was born, and for this I came into the world, to testify to the truth. Everyone who belongs to the truth listens to my voice." Pilate asked him, "What is truth?"

John 18:33-38

Another bus arrives and still more people pour from it into the piazza. This is not Rome. This is London. Busy London. Behind us Victoria Street, the Apollo Theatre and bustling business going on as usual. In front of us stands the neo-byzantine Cathedral of Westminster with its striking red-brick and Portland stone layers. The piazza we are standing in was not designed for this many people. The crowd has steadily grown from a couple of hundred when we arrived and now, squeezed into temporary pens, are at least two and a half thousand young people. Still more arrive.

I'm happy to be at the very back where I can observe the spectacle. Someone shouts "Viva Papa!" and there is laughter. In front of me is an assortment of young people, easily identified by their brightly coloured sweatshirts. Groups in green, yellow or blue, wearing the motif of a school or the name of a diocese. A chant starts up, "Benedetto, Benedetto". There is good humour, a sense of anticipation, and then Pope Benedict appears on the steps of the Cathedral to huge applause.

Next to me a group of families from the Philippines are ecstatic, jumping around, their hands clasped together like children at Christmas. Behind them a man in a dark suit stands shielding his eyes, straining to see Benedict give his speech. To my left a young American couple, tourists delighted to have stumbled on the event by accident, and behind them a man carrying his coffee, looking confused as if he is not sure what the fuss is all about. Among all this a stout man in a white t-shirt stands up and raises a banner tied to a piece of timber. As if to spoil the party he shouts, "Jesus Christ is my High Priest!" My first reaction is to smile. I'm not immediately sure what he is doing, until he shouts it again, this time more aggressively. It is obvious now that this man is uptight, anxious, determined to express himself. Anyone brave enough to take on a crowd is going to be convinced about themselves. He is not afraid to make his point and stand alone.

Next to him are two young girls in their early teens. From the look on their faces they are shocked by this man's announcement. They've barely noticed him before, but now with the Pope in his sights he is trying to make himself heard. He is a big man, towering over the girls. They look confused. On the banner the man's protest is written "Jesus Christ is my High Priest". The girls look at the man as if to say, "Why would you say that?" They are innocent of his objections.

This papal visit is not without its opponents. Accusations of unresolved child abuse in the Church, the cost of the state visit to the taxpayer, and Catholic teaching on contraception and homosexuality have all made national news in the run-up to this visit. Meanwhile, a secularist march is taking place nearby, led by prominent atheists calling upon the media to adopt a more critical view of the papal visit. None of that means much to the girls. They are excited and want to hear the Pope, who by now is giving a speech calling young people to prayer. The man with a banner does not share the opinions of the marching atheists. His contention runs much deeper than new atheism.

A ten-minute walk from here would take you to Westminster Abbey (often confused with Westminster Cathedral), the historic site of many coronations and the burial site of numerous kings and queens. At the eastern end of the Abbey, in tombs situated either side of Henry VII's chapel, are two cousins once removed: Mary Queen of Scots and Elizabeth I. These two women, much closer in death than life, represent a great divide: a rift which eventually led to Mary's brutal execution and caused continued pain for another four hundred years. One of the strongest objections between the two monarchs had its origins in where to situate authority. Today, the man with the banner is giving expression to a familiar old fear. His anxiety is about who is to be trusted and, like Elizabeth, he doesn't trust Rome.

One of the girls meekly approaches the man and says tentatively, "Jesus Christ is my High Priest too." She astounds me. Everyone else nearby is avoiding making eye contact with this man, let alone confronting a problem which put martyrs on both sides of the divide upon the scaffold. She is tackling an issue which led to schism across Europe and caused Christians to preach against each other. Surely such a divide, that split country from country and family from family, can't now be traversed by a thirteen-year-old girl?

He stops his shouting and looks down at the girl as if he too is surprised by her. Pointing towards the doors of the Cathedral he says, "That's your High Priest over there," and then he begins shouting again. I'm captivated by this girl. Turning to her friend as if to seek reassurance she asks, "Jesus is our High Priest too, isn't he?"

"Yes," says her friend, "I think he is."

The two of them have a brief conversation as to whether they had ever "done that" in religion classes. They look unsure what to say. The man is not waiting for them; he is back on task, waving his banner and shouting. The girls seem happy enough to let him get on with it, pulling the occasional face as if to signal to all around that he is not with them. His protest doesn't seem to dampen their enthusiasm. Neither does their enthusiasm seem to dampen his protest.

The Pope is receiving a gift on the steps of the piazza, and the crowd is chanting "Benedetto". The man's protest is no longer heard over the chant. As if admitting defeat and holding his banner with one hand he leans over, stretching to the floor to undo the straps of a small rucksack. His sandwich box falls out and he tries to reach it without dropping his banner. The lid of his lunchbox falls off and an apple rolls out. In this tight space, bending over and holding the banner poses him a problem. Seeing the plight of the man, the young girl says, "Give me your banner, and you can get your lunch." By now, the crowd is beginning to disperse and, keen to save his lunch from being trampled, he gives her the banner. Something wonderful is happening.

As everyone files past her out of the piazza, the girl is holding a banner which reads, "Jesus Christ is my High Priest". She has a radiant smile. In her hands, the banner is transformed from a protest to a statement of love. He begins to eat his lunch. Both of them are too close to see it, but I am watching the beginning of a healing. The last I heard him say before he left her was "Thank you sister," and I wondered if he had realised what he had just said? It was hardly what he came here to do.

▲ Making connections

The conversation between Jesus and Pilate is a deadly narrative. The enforcement of military law comes face to face with divine love. Love makes a fool of our need to be in control and Pilate is now on trial. His integrity is being tested by Jesus' innocence. Jesus, however, is vulnerable to violence because he will not become subject to the ways of the world. He does not allow his followers to retaliate. Exasperated, Pilate asks Jesus, "What is truth?", an ironic question coming from a judge. Pilate is looking at truth but he can't see it. Jesus answers Pilate's question with silence. Words will only lead to more words.

At a public meeting once, I witnessed a previous boss of mine being pilloried. People were accusing him of something for which he was not to blame. He said nothing to defend himself. After the meeting I remember asking why he didn't defend himself and he replied, "Sometimes David, it is better to be silent than to fight." There is wisdom here.

Words would not unite the man and the girl. Once our opinions become wrapped around our identities we can lose the ability to see truth. We have all known arguments when it became unclear what we were really arguing about. Where deeper damage has been done, we have to step into silence – not the silence that punishes people, but a deeper silence that refuses to give in to accusation. From there opportunities for love can emerge and this love demands that we lay down our weapons. When drawing swords fails, when arguments and counter arguments prevail, and when even the cleverest of ideas can't unite us, an act of kindness, no matter how small, begins to defeat fear, even when that fear has festered for four hundred years.

Conversation starters

- What is the best way to win an argument?
- Is retaliation ever a good response to conflict?

Chapter 9

Banana skins

Then the kingdom of heaven will be like this. Ten bridesmaids took their lamps and went to meet the bridegroom. Five of them were foolish, and five were wise. When the foolish took their lamps, they took no oil with them; but the wise took flasks of oil with their lamps. As the bridegroom was delayed, all of them became drowsy and slept. But at midnight there was a shout, "Look! Here is the bridegroom! Come out to meet him." Then all those bridesmaids got up and trimmed their lamps. The foolish said to the wise, "Give us some of your oil, for our lamps are going out." But the wise replied, "No! There will not be enough for you and for us; you had better go to the dealers and buy some for yourselves." And while they went to buy it, the bridegroom came, and those who were ready went with him into the wedding banquet; and the door was shut. Later the other bridesmaids came also, saying, "Lord, lord, open to us." But he replied, "Truly I tell you, I do not know you." Keep awake therefore, for you know neither the day nor the hour.

Matthew 25:1-13

Each year in the week after Easter, fifteen hundred people gather in a school in Ilfracombe, North Devon, for what is called "Celebrate". From all over Great Britain enthusiastic Christian families gather to mark their most important feast. Picture a car park full of people carriers, hundreds of teenagers bouncing around to Christian rock music, children doing finger-painting and a large hall full of people singing with gusto. The initial encounter is overwhelming, even off-putting, but stay with it and it is not hard to be affected by the energy of it all.

A team of technicians arrive four days before it all begins. They transform the school into a conference venue. The main gym is carpeted, hiding the markings of the badminton courts. The gym walls are covered by huge dark drapes which hang from ceiling to floor and are decorated by brightly painted banners. A temporary stage is set up, adorned by a spray of flowers. The musicians arrive with a multitude of amps, mics and a sound desk. Lighting is suspended on temporary gantries, the spotlights trained on the stage. Seating is packed in and positioned to conform to health and safety requirements. Classrooms are transformed into makeshift meeting rooms, book shops and prayer rooms. A temporary radio station provides broadcasts to delegates in the nearby holiday chalets. It is a remarkable feat of organisation and hard work.

Anyone who stands up regularly in front of large groups will tell you that a gathering of people, just like individuals, has a corporate personality. Some groups are on your side before they have sat down. They will come to the event like a purring cat, having decided it will be a good experience and proceeding to make it one. They laugh loudly, listen attentively, pray sincerely and applaud enthusiastically. Other groups are more reserved and resistant, perhaps because they are required by their employer to be there. They will arrive at the very last minute, fill seats from the back, fold their arms and perhaps bring in administration in the hope of working surreptitiously. The worse thing in these situations is to be introduced as "entertaining" because it is heard as a challenge: "Come on then... make me laugh."

Because I'm never certain of the response (I once had a teacher who sat in the front row and proceeded to mark assignments throughout my keynote), every time I walk to a podium or a lectern, or stand in front of a group large or small, I am nervous. No matter how well prepared, any teacher will tell you that all you need to ruin a good lesson is a wasp. Something can always throw you off course – like a failing projector bulb, a bishop on the front row, or a car alarm outside. Nervousness, I have come to realise, is a good thing. Adrenalin pumping around our bodies helps us to think quickly. It is more than biological, though. Nervousness shows respect. Usually, before I stand up, my mouth is dry, my palms sweaty, my mind racing. It would be wrong to be casual about moments like this.

For a speaker, Celebrate is a gift of a conference. The preparation is meticulous and the people gathering there are reading, thinking enthusiasts. They come with expectancy and trust. Cynicism is rare and gratitude is pervasive. There's no doubt about it – a speaker addressing an enthusiastic audience is in a very privileged position – but such an enthusiastic reception means you don't always see the slippery banana skin you're about to tread on.

This was not my first time speaking at Celebrate, and the warmth and welcome I'd received before allowed me the dangerous luxury of feeling relaxed. My preparation had been thorough. I'd consulted my Catechism, researched a few sources, prayed about the examples I'd use, written and rewritten. The combination of planning and the warmth of my reception made me sure I'd be okay. As I sat down near the podium I was unusually confident. During the course of the morning a group of musicians played their songs, a drama group performed a moving piece and there were announcements. The time for my keynote was drawing near. People were cheerful and attentive. Everyone was on my side, what could possibly go wrong?

Charles, the conference organiser, calls me to the stage. Leaving the front row of seats, I straighten my jacket, pick up my notes, check my lapel microphone is on, and walk up the steps to the stage. As I stand before this delightful group, my host says a short prayer and exits the stage. It is now me and them, a thousand people waiting in eagerness.

For a while everything seems to be going well. It is not unusual at this time of year for me to feel the early effects of hay fever. As I'm speaking I'm suddenly aware that my nose feels moist and I don't have a tissue. Perhaps if I brush my nose gently with the back of my finger I'll stem the flow and carry on. This I do, several times. For a while I think it's worked, but the runny nose sensation keeps coming back. I can sense restlessness and distraction in the front rows – perhaps it's my nose again. I try to wipe it discreetly.

It's important not to sniff because I'm wearing a lapel microphone, and for several minutes I've avoided looking down, thinking it will help to halt the flow. Finally I have to check my notes. To my horror, the pages are covered in blood. There's nothing readable – just a page of dark red. I try to carry on, but the flow is stronger than I realise. To make matters worse, the lectern I'm standing behind is transparent plastic and the blood is running off the pages and working its way slowly to the floor.

There's something about times like this when normal logic abandons you. In my panic I continue speaking as if the talk must go on. But most people are now watching a white shirt turn red and blood working its way down the lectern. The people on the front row are wide mouthed, aghast, stunned not by words of wisdom, but by a grotesque man who looks like he has been slugged in the face with a baseball bat. The lady directly in front of me looks as if she's at a crime scene. My hands, shirt and the lectern are smeared by blood. Attempting to wipe my face only rearranges the mess. "Someone stop him," I hear. "Please someone stop him." Finally, Charles the conference organiser returns to the stage: "It might be a good idea if you take a break," he says softly in my ear, with a hand on my shoulder. Returning to the front row I am covered by a fan-shaped mess extending from my chin the full width of my chest. My notes are useless.

After sitting calmly for a while, attended by a doctor who appeared from the crowd to offer help, I managed to get back to the lectern for a final ten minutes. The flow had been stemmed. Returning to my theme I was fully aware that no one was remotely interested. "What will be remembered," I thought to myself, "was a speaker with a nosebleed." It was true. If you're going to have a nosebleed, try not to have it in front of a thousand people while leaning on a transparent lectern. People will remember.

Making connections

There is a necessary nervousness in life around the things we consider important. Adrenalin is one indication that we value what we are about to do. There is a lovely paradox here. When you think you are ready you are not ready. When you carry a certain level of vulnerability about not being ready, you are ready. Being anxious for the things you do in the service of others is actually a sign of love.

Complacency is the banana skin because it reveals more than a lack of preparation. Being prepared in this sense is not about passing the school exam or trying harder. Being prepared biblically is about being in the right frame of mind. It is more about our disposition. When I forget the anniversary card, fail to telephone my mum, or start arriving late for meetings, I'm revealing a lack of appropriate care. When I stand up in front of people casually without a concern for their well-being, I'm showing a complacent disposition. To lead without nervousness is cavalier.

The ten bridesmaids are asleep. When they are awoken by the arrival of the bridegroom they are divided by their state of being. If I become complacent I wake up only to discover that I have lost the oil in my lamp. Jesus is not telling us to work harder, he is asking us if we care enough to be nervous.

Every now and again it is important to slip on a banana skin. It keeps us acute, awake to our need for God. Once I lose that I'm relying on myself, and when I do that, I get a nosebleed.

Conversation starters

- When do we take ourselves too seriously?
- What might be the merit in making a fool of ourselves?

Chapter 10

What the turkey taught us

*The kingdom of heaven is like treasure hidden
in a field, which someone found and hid; then in
his joy he goes and sells all that he has and buys
that field. Again, the kingdom of heaven is like a
merchant in search of fine pearls; on finding one
pearl of great value, he went and sold all that he
had and bought it. Again, the kingdom of heaven
is like a net that was thrown into the sea and
caught fish of every kind; when it was full, they
drew it ashore, sat down, and put the good into
baskets but threw out the bad. So it will be at
the end of the age. The angels will come out and
separate the evil from the righteous.*

Matthew 13:44-49

On 23 December 1977 at 4.23 p.m. precisely, the course of
my life changed dramatically. By 5 p.m. I would be
seeing things differently and the beginning of a new
world would be opening up to me. Most of our growing up takes
time, perhaps a lifetime, but in December 1977 I had to grasp a
few hard lessons pretty quickly. I was fifteen years old.

The purpose of our trip was to take a turkey to my sister who
would be working over Christmas in a hospital in Coventry. It is
hard to remember now what we were talking about, but our
conversation was interrupted. My dad had enough time to shout
only "What!" as the car coming towards us veered onto our side
of the road. At that time of year it is dark by 4.30 and it was the
headlights I recall most vividly, moving directly into our path.

Although what happened next took place in less than a few seconds, the terror enabled my brain to work extremely quickly and time effectively slowed down. For the next vital moments, everything happened in slow motion.

Both cars were travelling at around fifty miles an hour, which in terms of impact as the coroner later explained, was equivalent to hitting a stationary object at a hundred miles an hour. The other car landed on its roof, but ours was propelled backwards. As I lurched forward I felt the restraint of my seatbelt, and I saw the glass leave the windscreen in front of me. The immense sound of the impact was followed by a brief deafness. Mangled tangled metal, glass, the whirring of a redundant engine still functioning, shattered glass everywhere.

There are no other cars or people around. Looking to my right my dad is slumped on the steering wheel, groaning but unconscious. Stumbling from the car, I fall on the grass verge. A little dazed I come to my senses and stand up. For a second I comprehend the scene. What just happened? Moving towards the other car, its roof collapsed, I'm scared of what I might see. The vehicle is almost unrecognisable. I'm reluctant to get onto my knees and look. There is no cry for help. "My dad," I think, "help my dad". Moving to his door, the impact has made it impossible to open. Going back to my side of the car I lean over and try to manoeuvre him out of his seat. It is unclear to me what happens next; very suddenly the car is filled with blinding light. A man is helping me to get Dad out of the car and we lay him on the verge. A lorry driver has trained his headlights onto the crash scene. Sitting next to my dad, I become aware of people. There are now lots of people and the blue lights of an ambulance. We are put onto stretchers and carried into the ambulance. As I lie on my back I look through the skylight and semi-conscious I watch the glow of the street lights as we pass beneath them. By the time we reach the hospital I am paralysed from neck down, the consequence of extreme whiplash.

The other driver lost his life that night. My dad was left with a broken back, courtesy of the frozen turkey on the back seat not wearing a seat belt. All I suffered was two broken ribs and a diagonal burn which went from my shoulder to my waist, a reminder that the seatbelt had saved my life. Unaware of how my dad was faring on the operating table, I lay in my hospital bed unable to sit up. The nurses were not able to tell me about his progress, so asking for a pen, I wrote the strangest letter, a scrawl onto paper I could barely see, "Dad, I love you." The nurse told me she would give it to him. Years later we found it, in a drawer under his bed.

My dad could be a stubborn man. In moments like this, stubbornness becomes a virtue. At fifteen you can more easily absorb an impact like that. My dad, in his late forties, took the greater force, and his body the greater impact. Yet he was determined to return to work, to regain his life and to continue where he left off. This he did, never making the accident an excuse for anything. What he had to do was fight a recurring hip problem. My legacy was different; I had some growing up to do. At fifteen you feel immortal, invincible, and the future looks unending. It wasn't my life that felt in jeopardy. It was my dad's.

As a consequence of that incident, I became more appreciative of my parents. Normally at the age of fifteen you're more aware of what you don't get from your parents: freedom, money, attention, support, peer-group credibility. For most of us at fifteen, parents are an embarrassment. For me though, the possibility of losing them became very real and it led to an unusual appreciation for them. So much so, that somewhat foolishly I insisted that they came to my eighteenth birthday party, a party full of cheap spirits, vomit in the garden and prank telephone calls from college "friends".

As a young student, I remember calling my dad from university. I'm not sure what prompted the call but I was conscious of a need to say thank you, probably for his perseverance. It felt important to me to express a little gratitude for all that he had done in the background of my growing up. It should have been a father and son bonding moment. It wasn't. "Thank me for what I've done for you," he joked. "You've got no idea!" He was right; I had little idea of just how much they'd really done for me. "Look," he said almost reproachfully, "you don't have to thank me, I'm your dad. What I did, I did because I love you." Then he added a wonderful piece of wisdom: "If you learned anything from me," he said, "don't give it back to me, give it to your kids."

Making connections

The treasure in the field, the pearl of great value and the good catch of fish are not rewards, they are encounters with truth. When we find truth in our life we should cherish it as though we have found a pearl of great value. Our task is not to polish it and take it back to where we found it, but to make sure we hand it on. When our lives were threatened, I found a pearl first in the parents I took for granted, and then in what they taught me. Here the pearl my dad gave me was that under threat of losing him, I didn't have to repay him. For him, satisfaction came in giving to my children what he had given to me. That is what tradition is really for, to be passed forward, not returned.

Many people describe themselves as traditional when they mean old-fashioned. Tradition is often regarded as preferring things the way they were, recalling an experience and wishing we could go back in time. It is tempting to confuse nostalgia with tradition. A few years ago I found myself at the local refuse tip with a pram. Its padding was stained from years of chocolate biscuits. The frame was rusting from its incarceration in the garden shed. Standing beside it I could barely bring myself to add this pram to the pile of junk in front of me. The pram represented years of walking and talking to three small children. That time had gone and the pram was now junk. My longing for what that dear old pram represented was nostalgic and my desire to hold onto it was sentimental. Tradition is sometimes seen like that. Yearning for what was.

Imagine living in a world in which every generation starts only with itself. Imagine discounting all that has been revealed over the centuries by theologians, philosophers, historians, scientists and parents. At best we could only rediscover what we already once knew. My dad understood that. He didn't want to receive back the interest on what he had invested in me. He wanted me to give it to my children. That is tradition. When I act like him, think like him, do the things he did, he is alive. When I pass on to my children what he taught me, he is alive for ever. That is what tradition is really for, not to be preserved as jam but to be given away as a gift. Meanwhile, next time put a seatbelt on the turkey.

Conversation starters

- What have you learned to value most in life?
- Is it possible to give away the pearl of great value that life has given to us?

Chapter 11

Coming to my senses

Then he said, "There was a man who had two sons. The younger one said to his father, 'Father, let me have the share of the estate that will come to me.' So the father divided the property between them. A few days later, the younger son got together everything he had and left for a distant country where he squandered his money on a life of debauchery. When he had spent it all, that country experienced a severe famine, and now he began to feel the pinch; so he hired himself out to one of the local inhabitants who put him on his farm to feed the pigs. And he would willingly have filled himself with the husks the pigs were eating but no one would let him have them. Then he came to his senses and said, 'How many of my father's hired men have all the food they want and more, and here am I dying of hunger! I will leave this place and go to my father and say: "Father, I have sinned against heaven and against you; I no longer deserve to be called your son; treat me as one of your hired men."' So he left the place and went back to his father. While he was still a long way off, his father saw him and was moved with pity. He ran to the boy, clasped him in his arms and kissed him."

Luke 15:11-20 (New Jerusalem Bible)

As an experienced teacher I thought I'd be quite useful with teenagers, but children really confused me. If I tried to discipline them I'd go from giving mixed messages and being inconsistent, to being scary and frightening.

It was hard to tell the difference. I've got one of those very expressive faces which is useful in commanding silence in a corridor-full of teenagers, but not so good with a three-year-old who won't eat his mashed potato.

As she walked up that aisle I really thought I knew my wife to be. But when we had children I saw a completely new side to her, something I'd not seen before. What so impressed me about Alison's parenting skills was her resourcefulness. It was the way she was able to get our children to change their behaviour without causing post-traumatic stress syndrome. Shaking their head to say "no" as she tried to insert a spoon, she would suddenly pull out a plastic zoo animal and shout "Look!", and the mouth would open and in would go the spoon. Brilliant. Where did she learn that? As the boys would fight over the first go on the slide, she'd pick up a snail and call them over and before you knew it the conflict was forgotten. Then she'd say, "Now, who is going to look after the snail, and who is first on the slide?" She'd give them two good options instead of one. To this day, whether it was cooking jam tarts, taking them to football training, helping with algebra or just listening to them, I marvel at just how well she attended to their needs without spoiling them.

Parenting on good days is filled with laughter, discovery and the stuff you don't realise you'll miss one day. Unfortunately there's another side to it – with very small children it can be incredibly boring. Disturbed sleep night after night, together with the endless repetition of a toddler's favourite game, is enough to drive an adult insane. Even Walt Disney's classic *The Jungle Book* is mind-numbing after six or seven watches. In a world of primary-coloured objects, basic tunes, clapping and standing on one leg, it all lacks subtlety. For some parents the early years can descend into dull, dreary isolating routine.

Monday evenings after work I'd head off for five-a-side football. Sometimes we'd have a pint in the bar afterwards. As I pulled up outside our home the children would see the headlights, their faces pressed at the window. As I opened the door they'd run to me in their pyjamas and I was quickly throwing them onto the sofa and tickling them. Their laughter was uplifting. "Don't get them too hyper," I'd hear Alison say, having tried to calm them down before bedtime. Then I'd take them upstairs and tell them a story. Afterwards Ali and I would share that brief reprieve that comes between tidying up their mess and falling asleep on the sofa.

For Alison, meeting in the daytime with other mums helped, but it wasn't a social life. So it was good to hear that Ali had arranged to go out for a drink with a few friends and that I could take over to give her a little breathing space. There is plenty of adult stimulus for me at work and what Ali needed most was a distraction from herself as a mum. She needed a conversation that wasn't about baby grows or childcare arrangements.

As she left for a night out, I began my "evening with dad" routine. We built towers made of bricks and then sent them crashing to the floor. We found an old cardboard box and turned it into a shop and then it became a fort to defend. We played a game called "Get around the house without touching the floor". We had egg and chips and watched *A Bug's Life*. We lit a fire in the garden and made sparks fly from the embers. Then they had a drink and went to bed. They fell asleep listening to another of my war stories.

Downstairs again I turn to the ironing. Not much of it, but a pile all the same. Working my way through it, I'm getting ready to put my feet up, relax and bring to an end all the things that are on a little list Alison has written for me. As she walks through the door she will arrive home to find bathed children fast asleep, a tidy kitchen, the ironing done, and me asleep on the sofa in front of some late-night dross on the television. Most importantly of all, she'll be grateful. She's had a good night out and the chores are done. Turns out I'm a good husband after all.

The following Monday morning I was back at work chatting to some colleagues about how the weekend went. "Fine," I said, "I did a spot of babysitting on Friday night – Ali had a night out with the girls." "Babysitting?" said one of them inquisitively, "I thought they were your kids?" and they all laughed.

As I sat at my desk my colleague's words cut through me into a space only I go. She was right, they are my kids. In a moment of sadness I recognised in myself something I didn't like. For a few years I had been behaving as if each time I looked after the kids or helped around the house I was doing my wife a favour. In my imagination I had managed to content myself that somehow I was noble and enlightened for lending a hand. What kind of foolishness is a father who is doing his wife a favour by being a dad to his children? To my embarrassment I almost expected her to come home that night and be grateful. Night after night, week after week I would get home to see a skilful devoted mother loving her children and never once did I imagine she was doing me a favour. Why should it work one way and not the other? My dad told me that there would be moments like this; when to be a man would be to acknowledge that you have got some growing up to do. "Grow up," I thought. I'm their dad, not their babysitter.

Making connections

Luke 15 is one of my favourite chapters in the entire Bible and consists of several stories about losing and finding, the lost sheep found, the lost coin found, the lost son found. In one of the most famous stories Jesus told, we find a wayward son too proud to come home, deciding to return not as a son but as a servant. He sits among the pigs and finally acknowledges to himself his state of disgrace. In his defeat he comes "to his senses". In coming to his senses he is found again. In losing his dignity he finds his purpose. This simple little phrase, "he came to his senses", is the lynchpin of the whole story. This is the pivotal moment. From then on he is rediscovering himself. He is no longer lost because he knows where to go. He's going home. He's going back to the Father.

Coming to your senses is crucial for a disciple. It is the moment in the middle of a full-blown argument when you hear that quiet voice in the back of your head which says, "Actually, David, what you are doing here is wrong." It is a cold, daunting place where you confront your own darkness. The Church calls it an examination of conscience and most of us don't choose to go there often.

Sometimes we pretend to go there. When a teenager says sorry and exaggerates the word while rolling their eyes, they are apologising but they haven't come to their senses. When a child says sorry hurriedly and repeatedly to avoid a punishment, they too are not coming from the place of the senses. When a politician apologises after being caught, the apology is generally an attempt at damage limitation. These are all tactics. They are not examples of coming to your senses. Everyone knows when an apology comes from the senses, because it truly hurts in the telling.

I'd loved my children from the moment I saw them, but in one of my bleakest growing up moments it turned out that in our family it wasn't the son who'd gone missing. It was the dad. Busily doing all the right things for the wrong reasons. I'm aware that there is much growing up still to do, but coming to your senses is the beginning of hope, not the depth of despair, and while it is painful at the time, there is a better person emerging.

Conversation starters

- Do we have an inner voice which tells us we are wrong?
- What does it mean, to come to our senses?

Chapter 12

Letting it go

When Jesus saw the crowds, he went up the mountain; and after he sat down, his disciples came to him. Then he began to speak, and taught them, saying: "Blessed are the poor in spirit, for theirs is the kingdom of heaven. Blessed are those who mourn, for they will be comforted. Blessed are the meek, for they will inherit the earth. Blessed are those who hunger and thirst for righteousness, for they will be filled. Blessed are the merciful, for they will receive mercy. Blessed are the pure in heart, for they will see God. Blessed are the peacemakers, for they will be called children of God. Blessed are those who are persecuted for righteousness' sake, for theirs is the kingdom of heaven. Blessed are you when people revile you and persecute you and utter all kinds of evil against you falsely on my account. Rejoice and be glad, for your reward is great in heaven, for in the same way they persecuted the prophets who were before you."

Matthew 5:1-12

There is a certain madness somewhere inside me. A meeting goes badly and while driving home I start rehearsing what I wish I'd said in the exchange. In my mind I'm being very reasonable. Rethinking the conversation, words start coming out of my mouth even though I am on my own. I'm talking to myself at the wheel. To compound my madness I give my adversary their responses, as though I know how they would have responded. In effect I'm having a row with myself. This only feeds my anxiety. When I pull up outside my home I'm worse off for the imaginary encounter. These mind games, which start with hurt and frustration, only end up compounding the misunderstanding. Emails can be like that if we click "Send" too soon. The same goes for road rage.

My morning journey to work used to take me through the Devon countryside and Exeter suburbs into the city centre. Like many older cities, Exeter's roads are not designed to accommodate the weight of cars and rush hour – the most inaccurate definition I know – progresses at snail's pace. By 8 a.m. the major arteries are clogging up. Fortunately, after some experimenting, I found a shortcut through a housing estate. I worked out that it would take a good ten minutes (thirty-nine hours a year) off my journey. The only problem was a T-junction at the far end, which meant crossing a busy main road, taking my life in my hands. Whatever happens, I would say to myself, don't stall now!

When it rains all the parents who normally walk their children to school get into their cars and the traffic jams are even longer. One such morning, along with a number of other drivers, I decide to use the shortcut and head through the winding roads of the housing estate. When we arrive at the perilous T-junction, a large black four-by-four is waiting for a gap in the traffic. It is a beautiful new model and I can't help but covet it. I'm tapping the steering wheel as I listen to the morning news. This is my world, my little rarefied, invincible, private space, as I prepare myself for the day ahead.

The car behind me pulls up abruptly, as if he hadn't seen me until the very last minute. The screech of his breaks is audible over my radio. In my wing mirror he looks as if he is having an argument, but no one is in the car with him. He gestures that I'm in his way. Silencing the radio and focusing in my mirror, it's clear to me that he's either late or worried about something – probably both. I choose to ignore his gesture – it's probably better if I don't look. Suddenly, for some reason thinking that it might speed things up, he hits the car horn twice and, after a pause, a third time. Now I can't ignore him. In the mirror I raise my hands. "Where can I go?" I gesture. There's a car in front of me. What am I supposed to do, shunt it forward into traffic? The horn is meant to sound a warning, but here it feels like a weapon. What is happening to us that we treat each other like this?

In the car in front of me I see a woman trying to focus on her manoeuvre. The noise behind her just adds to the pressure on her. Like her I don't appreciate the frustration of the driver behind as he hits his horn a fourth time. She must time her exit according to her own judgement and her thoughts must be on making her decision in her own time. The car horn is an angry rebuke. To my surprise, she gestures at me, taking out her anger on me. She mouths "What do you want?" and I realise that she doesn't know where the sound is coming from. She thinks it's me. Attempting to explain I start to gesture, pointing behind me. "It's him," I insist, holding my hands in the air as if to say, "He's lost the plot."

She doesn't look remotely placated by my gesture, and I suddenly realise that I'm pointing at the queue behind me and she thinks I'm saying, "Look at all the traffic building up behind me." This only makes things worse. I'm being wrongly accused by the woman in front because of the impatience of the man behind. Misunderstandings on all sides.

Finally she makes her move and drives across the road successfully, but to my surprise rather than heading off on her way, she pulls up. From the far side of the busy street she puts her window down and glares at me accusingly. She holds her hands out to me as if to say, "Well, you wanted my attention, now you have it." I'm looking directly across the street at her, cars speeding between us; I can't escape her stare. And still, the guy behind me looks as though he's about split his shirt with Hulk-like annoyance. I'm sitting in my car, accused from all sides. All this blame before I've even got to work.

As I take my moment to cross the road I slow down to pass the woman. As clearly as I can, I lean across the passenger seat and say, "I'm sorry," and point to the side of my head as if to suggest that I'm daft. This time, instead of retaliating, perhaps I can do something better. As though her anger were a helium balloon I could take it and drive off with it until I am capable of letting it go. Instead of feeding the misunderstanding, for once I could absorb it. At least then I might not discover later that day that I am angry. As I drive away I say to myself "Let it go," and neither anger nor imaginary conversation have got the better of me.

Making connections

Most adventure movies start with an injustice of some kind, then proceed with a journey of discovery and finish with an act of vengeance. The source of the injustice is destroyed at the end and we are satisfied. When injustice happens in real life it rarely works that way. We are often left with a feeling that the situation is unresolved and we have to deal with letting it go. Peter gives voice to this frustration, "Lord, if another member of the church sins against me, how often should I forgive? As many as seven times?" (Matthew 18:21). Implicit in his question is a yearning for a time when forgiveness will be dispensed with and he can give his adversaries what they really deserve.

The Beatitudes used to annoy me a bit. They don't appear to satisfy the way the movies do. For a long time I wasn't sure why anyone would want these attitudes: to be poor in spirit, mourning, meek, hungering for righteousness, merciful, pure in heart, peace-making, or persecuted and maligned. Jesus gives each a reward, but as life experiences they looked unattractive. Until in fact I discovered that each of them can be transformative. On a good day, they have a capacity to repair and restore in a way that vengeance doesn't. Often I'm too self-absorbed or vulnerable to get it right. Just occasionally I can be big enough to accept these dispositions as a means to absorb the misunderstanding or anger I see around me. Adopting the Beatitudes can equip us to soak up pain and stress, rather than giving it back in kind. They become a source of healing.

Being human involves living with misunderstanding even while we are driving to work. In my response, though, I have a choice; I can return the insult, or if I'm not in pieces myself, I can absorb it, carry it, and in time just let it go. People often say they want to make the world a better place. The Beatitudes might be a good place to start.

Conversation starters

- How long do we hold on to resentment, anger or irritation?
- What are the best ways to respond to people who are offensive?

Chapter 13

Naked at St Anne's

They came to Jericho. As he and his disciples and a large crowd were leaving Jericho, Bartimaeus son of Timaeus, a blind beggar, was sitting by the roadside. When he heard that it was Jesus of Nazareth, he began to shout out and say, "Jesus, Son of David, have mercy on me!" Many sternly ordered him to be quiet, but he cried out even more loudly, "Son of David, have mercy on me!" Jesus stood still and said, "Call him here." And they called the blind man, saying to him, "Take heart; get up, he is calling you." So throwing off his cloak, he sprang up and came to Jesus. Then Jesus said to him, "What do you want me to do for you?" The blind man said to him, "My teacher, let me see again." Jesus said to him, "Go; your faith has made you well." Immediately he regained his sight and followed him on the way.

Mark 10:46-52

Situated in one of the more socially deprived neighbourhoods of Nottingham was a small Franciscan community. The Catholic school next to the friary was a meeting place for the many parents and grandparents who gathered there twice a day to drop off and pick up their children. Having worked in many more affluent communities I was pleased to be asked by the Friar to work in St Anne's. "Many parents here rely on their school but have little connection to the parish," said the Friar. We need some way to meet these parents and connect with them." He expressed an earnest desire to draw a few younger families into the life of his ageing parish.

We agreed our strategy. Since many of the parents were not in full-time employment, we would offer something for them immediately after they had dropped their children off at school. We would run a series of talks in a nearby pub, owned by a sympathetic landlord who was a parishioner in the parish. The pub was considered more familiar and less threatening than the church hall. Tiny children would be cared for in a crèche in the bar area, while I would work with the parents in the lounge next door. It was a good plan, sensitive to the lives of the people we were trying to support.

Arriving early I prepared my projector and screen and dutifully distributed handouts around the tables. I had tea, coffee and biscuits at the ready and a warm smile to greet them on arrival. I needn't have worried whether anyone would turn up. As the school bell rang to announce the beginning of the school day, the bar and lounge filled up quickly. The parents and grandparents who arrived were all women, pleased to have breathing space and childcare provided. The room was full of their raw energy, gossip and laughter. This was a space they felt at home in. Soon a few of the women had lit cigarettes and the ceiling was thick with smoke. The smoke descended slowly in a horizontal blanket until we were all enveloped in a dim fog. These were the last days when cigarette smog was still legal in pubs.

"If I could just have your attention," I said loudly. "My name is David and I have been invited by the head teacher to lead these sessions. We can use the time to look at common concerns we share as parents and to see if there are ways the parish can help us. I have prepared some material here to get us going and we will see what emerges."

I turned towards my slides to begin my presentation, but by now I had lost them. They continued talking to each other as if I had just interrupted something more pressing. Two women near me concentrated on my every word, but when I asked them their names I discovered they didn't have a word of English between them.

"What was I doing wrong?" I asked myself as I drove home, agonising over good intentions lost somewhere in the doing. "Perhaps it is the 'doing' that is the problem," I thought. Perhaps another approach was needed.

In spite of my effort rather than because of it, they all happily arrived a week later. This time I left the projector in the boot of my car and replaced it with a flip chart and marker pens. Feeling naked without a plan, I asked them, "What would you like to discuss?" I was poised ready to note down their answers on my big piece of A1-size paper.

There was a mixture of sympathetic attention, bemusement and a very long pause. "Come on… come on," I thought, "there has to be a something in there, a reason for us to meet."

"Sex!" came a sharp reply. "Let's talk about sex," and there was laughter.

"Yes," said another. "Let's talk about sex."

Reluctantly I turned away from my empty flip chart and put my marker pen down.

"Okay," I said, acknowledging to myself that this was probably no more than an effort to embarrass me. "Let's talk about sex, as the only man in the room I might learn something."

They laughed again. What followed was a deluge of stories about men. Some raucous stories about men, but mostly negative stories about men.

At home that night I took a look in mirror. It wasn't just the projector that was wrong. I was wrong. There I am, standing in front of them suited and polished, looking like the man that comes to their house to collect the rent.

"Next week," I thought, "I'll lose the tie and the flip chart."

Perhaps being professional is not the same as looking professional.

These women talked about sex for the next three weeks. It wasn't specifically about sex so much as relationships, and it was raw and truthful. The conversation lacked subtlety but it also avoided all the pretences that can come with a higher education. The stories were mainly about the men who had let some of these women down. Men who in their opinion had not grasped the responsibility of fatherhood, or had not grown up at all.

"My old man says all the right things," said one woman. "Then he's gone again".

She didn't seem able to decide who she loathed more, her husband or herself.

Week four, and I was greeted outside the pub: "How is the course going?" asked the Friar. I realised that we had not begun to cover the issues he hoped to address. The Friar had the parents' intentions at heart and cared for them, but he also hoped that the course would prompt a return to his church. We were still a long way from that. By now we were building up a slowly emerging sense of solidarity, more between them than with me. They had a way of empathising with each other which I admired. Not the sort of empathy you receive from training. Other signs of progress were there. The two Polish women sitting at the front had gone to the trouble of finding a translator. They'd agreed as a group not to smoke because of an asthma sufferer. These women were talking in a large group with a growing interest in a single conversation.

The thought of me now disrupting the process with an overt religious agenda troubled me. By now the whole experience seemed more theirs than mine. Should a religious agenda surface, it seemed to me that it needed to be theirs. To me it was now almost inappropriate to offer them what seemed like a hidden agenda. Driving home I had a new anxiety. It disturbed me that I was now more nervous and embarrassed about praying with them than I was about talking about sex.

As the final session came toward its end I said tentatively, "If anyone would like to stay on a few minutes, I'm going to suggest we pray about the sort of things we have been saying. Please understand that it is really okay to stay or go."

There was a silence but remarkably no one moved. Not one of them. Nervously I lit a candle and positioned it on the floor in the middle of the lounge, a place where they normally found solace in a drink or two.

"Enjoy our silence," I said, hoping to reassure them that we had all said enough.

"If you want to, you can say anything to God, aloud or in silence, you don't have to make speeches."

A silence followed. I didn't imagine that anyone would pray aloud, and then to my surprise one of the women began to say, "Dear Lord... ".

There was a silence again. She was using words she had learned as a child, but then her prayer quietly roared its way out of a world-weary heart.

"My life is hard," and she began to weep. That was all she could say to God, "My life is hard." Then a few of the others began to weep as if she had said all that needed to be said. They didn't need context or explanation, they understood each other. This was indeed becoming holy ground and all I needed to do was get out of the way. This was prayer of the deepest kind, for it came from the most wounded of hearts.

Discreetly and not for effect, I took off my shoes. Over the years I have learned to do that. When something powerful happens, it is a good idea to take off the shoes and feel the ground. There is something bigger than us here and the ground... as Moses was taught before the burning bush, keeps us grounded.

Making connections

There is so much going on in the short story of poor Bartimaeus. Jesus is at his most popular and so the crowds engulf him. Bartimaeus must shout from a discarded place, the roadside at the city gate. Jesus cannot see him. In his shouting, he gives Jesus a title "Son of David". This tells Jesus that despite Bartimaeus' lack of physical sight, he has the insight to see who Jesus really is. What follows is astonishing.

Jesus asks a blind beggar what he wants. If I was one of Jesus' followers I'd have interrupted at this moment and offered Jesus some advice. "Jesus," I'd say politely, "he's blind, he's a beggar, and he's regarded as lost to God and Israel for both those reasons." It would have been obvious to me that he needed healing and then restoration before the Law of Moses. Then he could resume his place in Jewish society and start to earn his own living. Simple as that.

Jesus asks a question first. It is an enormous discipline to ask first. We are often at our most useless when we do not ask questions because we think we know the answers. There is nothing quite as suffocating as someone doing our thinking for us. People in power, politicians, religious leaders, and we parents can forget to ask.

Jesus does not impose his will upon people. He is not manipulative or coercive. In response to the insight of Bartimaeus, Jesus rewards him with sight itself, but only after he answers the request, "Let me see again." Good teachers know that the first act of mercy is to have a good question; the second is to have a good answer. One of the first lessons in discipleship is to lose all assumptions about people. That is perhaps why I found myself in a room full of women, talking about sex and why, I suspect, I'll have to learn this lesson again. Many times.

Conversation starters

- In what ways do we prejudge situations before we understand them?
- Where do we notice a need for more careful listening?

Chapter 14

The disappearance of Paolo

Now there was an Ethiopian eunuch, a court official of the Candace, queen of the Ethiopians, in charge of her entire treasury. He had come to Jerusalem to worship and was returning home; seated in his chariot, he was reading the prophet Isaiah. Then the Spirit said to Philip, "Go over to this chariot and join it." So Philip ran up to it and heard him reading the prophet Isaiah. He asked, "Do you understand what you are reading?" He replied, "How can I, unless someone guides me?" And he invited Philip to get in and sit beside him. Now the passage of the scripture that he was reading was this: "Like a sheep he was led to the slaughter, and like a lamb silent before its shearer, so he does not open his mouth. In his humiliation justice was denied him. Who can describe his generation? For his life is taken away from the earth." The eunuch asked Philip, "About whom, may I ask you, does the prophet say this, about himself or about someone else?" Then Philip began to speak, and starting with this scripture, he proclaimed to him the good news about Jesus.

Acts 8:27-35

Market Harborough, a quaint eighteenth-century coaching town nestled in the heart of England, was an uneventful place to grow up. Surrounded by rolling green countryside, attractive red-brick villages and charming little pubs it was the sort of small-town location that went largely unnoticed by anyone except its inhabitants. Not much happened there that would draw the attention of outsiders. The local papers carried the usual mixture of arguments about car parking fees or planning applications for house extensions, but back in the 70s you could be forgiven for thinking that in Harborough at least, the future looked pretty much like the past.

The community was also home to Irish, Polish and Italian immigrants who had settled there in the 1950s and 60s. Paolo, like so many children of immigrant parents, had to deal with a gap between his life at home and life in the neighbourhood. Even in the sleepiest of towns, the gap between home and street could be difficult to navigate. For children like Paolo, it led to an inclination to keep their head down and live in the shadows at school. This gentle, timid boy had no desire to stand out and be noticed, especially in front of a crowd.

Looking back on it now I think that, for the shy Paolo, the pain of being in the limelight must have reached new levels when, for one hour a week as a reluctant altar server, he would accompany the priest into the church sanctuary in front of two hundred and fifty people, much to the delight of his devout Catholic mother. She would pray in earnest every time she saw him in this role, that Paolo might one day have a calling to become a priest.

Being an altar boy involves dressing in a cassock and attending to the needs of the priest as he presides at Mass. It involves ringing bells, carrying cruets, processing with candles, all highly choreographed. In the Catholic liturgy, actions are not spontaneous or casual. Being an altar server means knowing where to be, what to do and when to do it. It requires rehearsing.

Because it all felt very serious, there was room for occasional childish comedy. When laughter is inappropriate, it is so much harder to resist. A woman wearing a long dress knows to lift up her hem when she's going up stairs. But if you don't know that, it's quite possible to walk up the inside of your altar server's cassock until you're no longer able to stand upright. Occasionally a boy would end up halfway up the front of his cassock, reduced to an L-shape, much to the hilarity of the other servers. Reversing out of the situation was just as embarrassing. Even more amusing to ten-year-olds was the combination of candles with cassocks. Every now and again someone would catch fire and not realise until they smelt burning cotton. Incidents like these became the stuff of legend and camaraderie.

As children we didn't understand a great deal about why we did what we did; we just waited for the prompt and responded accordingly. The repetition was helpful. As long as everything happened in the correct sequence everyone knew what to do. Variety is risky if you don't have a firm grasp of the principles behind the actions. If anything disrupted the usual sequence quiet panic would set in among the boys. Surprises didn't go down well, and the congregation much preferred ceremonial familiarity.

One sunny Sunday morning, Paolo and I processed into the sanctuary with the priest for the start of the nine o'clock service. The sun cast a cascade of coloured light through the stained glass. We bowed and assumed our positions in front of the altar. The scene was just as it was every Sunday morning. Catholics generally sit in the same place every week even though they would never claim it as their own. On this Sunday as any other, the pews were full of the usual people in their usual places. It is nine o'clock on Sunday morning. Everyone is in their stations. The universe is safe. Mass can begin.

There was an unscheduled pause. Something was distracting the priest. Beckoning Paolo up the steps towards him, he had something to say. This was not normal procedure, and it was easy to see Paolo's anxiety. He glanced nervously at me as if to say: "What's going on?" The priest was an imposing man, broad shouldered with silver hair. He was also an intense, intelligent man who found trivia difficult. Much admired by the community, he was more suited to adults than children. When presiding in the service he could be especially directive, which only exacerbated our anxiety to get it right.

Summoning Paolo to his side, the priest murmured a few instructions which were barely audible to Paolo. Paolo said quietly, "Pardon?" The priest explained again. Paolo looked concerned, his forehead furrowed, his face crestfallen. He bowed before the altar reverently and walked off the sanctuary to attend to the errand he had been assigned. He walked past the gathered assembly and into the sacristy at the side of the church. A cold dark room where we robed, the sacristy contained floor-to-ceiling cupboards, a sink, and many of the cruets and items needed for services. With Paolo gone, the priest and people waited patiently for his return in order to continue with Mass.

The gathering waited, standing in silence. Seconds stretch at times like these. No time at all begins to seem like for ever. The faces of two hundred and fifty onlookers displayed kindly patience. Back at home, many Sunday roasts were cooking on a low heat. There was a quiet restlessness you see in big crowds which has a way of telling you to move on. But we didn't. We kept waiting. People cast polite looks to each other. A curiosity hung over the assembled.

Finally, his patience wearing thin, the priest summoned me forward just as he had Paolo. Nervously proceeding to the priest's chair I said, "Yes Father," waiting for his instruction. He whispered, "The tabernacle key is not here next to the tabernacle where it should be, go in the sacristy and fetch it."

There are a number of things we had to do before the service, which included lighting candles and putting the tabernacle key on the altar so that at the appropriate moment the priest could open the tabernacle to bring out the consecrated bread for Communion. Like Paolo before, I bowed to the altar, exited the sanctuary and made my way to the sacristy next door as I was told. The crowd looked on.

Once in the sacristy I ran to the small wooden draw which contained the key for the tabernacle. Carefully opening the draw I found to my amazement the key, positioned on the cloth in its usual place, lying there in readiness. Taking it from the draw I began to make my way back into the church. The immediate predicament was resolved, but then it struck me that my friend was nowhere to be seen. The key was there, but no Paolo. As quietly and quickly as I could, I went from one room to another calling his name in urgent whisper, but I couldn't find him. Where on earth was he? What was he doing? Why didn't he fetch the key as instructed?

By now the organist had started up a hymn in the church as if to make more use of the time. My head was telling me to go back and give the priest the key but my heart was concerned for the whereabouts of my pal. Then I noticed the coat hanger upon which Paolo's cassock was hanging, neatly ironed as if it had never been used. I ran out into the bright sunshine to see that his bicycle, normally fastened to the lamp post outside the church door, had gone. It didn't take Sherlock Holmes to deduce that my good-natured companion had in fact gone home. Paolo had taken flight and got away from there as quickly as he possibly could. He had done a runner. So I returned to the sanctuary where two hundred and fifty people were waiting. As I placed the key on the altar, Father said "Thank you," and we continued with the Mass. My mind was distracted completely by thoughts about Paolo. What on earth just happened?

Making connections

What we don't know tends to frighten us more than what we do know. Most horror films lose their grip once the beast of the story is revealed. Anticipation is almost always worse than the unfolding of events, and so the waiting room rather than the consultation is where we're more anxious. "What if... ?" is a frightening thought.

When Philip met the Ethiopian he asked him a good question, "Do you understand what you are reading?" "How can I?" he replied, "unless someone guides me?" He asked for help. Once we have knowledge we can begin to hope; once we understand the symptoms we can begin to respond with courage. It is the not knowing which disables us more than the knowing. Even the smallest detail is significant if not knowing it renders us incapable.

Not knowing where the key was kept was enough to frighten poor Paolo onto his bike away from his humiliation. Like us all, he couldn't bear to reveal what he didn't know. When we don't know, we become afraid of displaying our ignorance and we may choose to run away. As far as I am aware, Paolo never returned as a server and I was too young to understand why.

In a speech about education Cardinal Hume once said, "Education is holy". By that he didn't mean that learning about religion is holy. He meant that all education is holy, including why ice floats, how to warm muscles before a race, learning French verbs, how to hill-start a car or where keys are kept. He was teaching us that ignorance generates fear. Education on the other hand leads people to become more fully alive; its fruits include dignity and confidence. When I have greater knowledge it becomes a more challenging world, not a fearful one.

Church schools were inspired not only to help people get good jobs, as important as that may be, but also because the dignity and worth of people is elevated by learning. There is far more to all this than getting children and teachers through all the tests. Good schools get it. The more I know, the more I know about who I am, who God is, and who God is calling me to be. No knowledge is excluded from this. Education is holy, because knowledge is an antidote to fear, and fear thrives in the absence of God.

Spare a thought for Dr Yvette Cloete, a paediatrician who lived in South Wales. Vigilantes vandalised her home and painted the word "Paedo" across her front door. Police confirmed that the attack was prompted by confusion over the words "paedophile" and "paediatrician". Dr Cloete confirmed that she left the house after the attack which she found very distressing. Ignorance generates fear.

It has taken me a long time to learn to ask for help, but it is daring to ask that gives rise to holiness. The important thing is to keep looking for the key, no matter how foolish we feel.

Conversation starters

- Why are people reluctant to ask for help?
- What are the best ways to build confidence?

Chapter 15

Are we there yet?

He also said, "The kingdom of God is as if someone would scatter seed on the ground, and would sleep and rise night and day, and the seed would sprout and grow, he does not know how. The earth produces of itself, first the stalk, then the head, then the full grain in the head. But when the grain is ripe, at once he goes in with his sickle, because the harvest has come."

Mark 4:26-29

England is sliced up by over four thousand miles of narrow canals. In the short period that lasted between the building of the first factories and the development of the steam railways, there was a short-lived era of canals. These canals enabled long narrowboats pulled by horses to carry coal, potash and lime. When the railways came, the canals became redundant. Today holidaymakers take advantage of these beautiful waterways to meander slowly across this green and pleasant land. Two hundred and fifty years after the Irish navvies dug these canals, I am enjoying a narrowboat trip with a few good friends on a very hot weekend in June.

Although it is early morning, the sun beats down upon the rolling Warwickshire countryside. The rising heat from the warm earth distorts the distant views of yellow rape fields and unripe corn. The gnats dash every which way in frantic flight, but every other living creature is slow and listless, conserving energy for the sapping summer's day ahead. The air is laden with summer scent, and the signs of vibrant life are everywhere. Sitting on the roof of the canal barge it is indeed easy to appreciate how good life can sometimes be. Nature's canvas unfolds before me around every twist and turn in the course of the contour-hugging canal. The sole extent of my responsibility on this lazy day is to flip the top from a bottle of beer. It is hard to imagine a more perfect scene.

To preserve these canals and the banked earth which contains them, narrowboats are limited to a speed of just four miles per hour. Moving faster than walking pace, but only just, every view emerges slowly to delight the senses. Each meander in the canal is anticipated with time to spare. The willow casts its drooping branches into the water, and for several moments you anticipate their caress before the boat brushes them aside. There are few sudden surprises. With the ponderous rhythm of the engine, and the gentle motion of the boat, the mind is forced to slow down. At four miles an hour the brain is treated to a feast of detail: moorhens nesting in the reeds, the reflection off a fisherman's flask, the smell of bacon from a frying pan, a dog barking in a distant farmyard, the single brush stroke of a distant cirrus cloud being the only blemish in an otherwise pale blue sky.

In the distance I see a motorway bridge, a huge leviathan built on tall concrete pillars and stretching wide across the landscape as if cast down by some imposing giant. It is visible for an hour before we plunge into its shadow. The unremitting sound of tyre on tarmac drones like a swarm of bees. As we approach the bridge the sound becomes more intrusive. This twentieth-century landmark disturbs our hazy day. We are at the Watford Gap, a stretch of motorway with six of the busiest traffic lanes in the British Isles. Aligned with it, a busy railway line and another road, and low down beneath this busy transport hub snakes our serpentine canal. You would never know it was there unless you chose to ride on the barge. For the oblivious travellers on the motorway above, we proceed unnoticed.

Captivated by this impressive testament to modern engineering I was struck by its strange and abrupt beauty. There were no subtle tones, no soft edges, just hard lines – reliable, indefatigable, uncompromising lines. These concrete pillars supported millions of vehicles moving people and goods from one place to another. You could never question the motorway's purpose or doubt its effectiveness. If in need of the emergency services to get me to a hospital I wouldn't choose to travel via the canal. The concrete artery above me needed no qualification. Motorways are efficient. Canals are not. There was something perplexing about this graphic example of eighteenth-century dogged determination meeting twentieth-century urgency.

As we travelled beneath the din of tyre on tarmac, I had a chilling thought: "Is the whole world late for something?" The cost-effective, performance-driven, incentive-motivated, pragmatic efficiency of the road above me looked like madness from the roof of my dawdling canal barge. After just a few hours travelling at four miles per hour, the canal looked and felt like sanity. Were we really meant to live at the speed of sound?

It was then that I was struck by the real casualty of the motorway. "When you are on it," I thought to myself, "it doesn't feel fast." That is the great lie of the motorway. Because everyone is travelling so fast together, there is no sense of speed. Looking across the traffic lanes at fellow travellers you could be forgiven for imagining there is little in the way of movement. The background is a blur, but what doesn't appear to be moving so quickly are the vehicles. Surprisingly, since everyone is travelling at such a rapid pace, there is less sense of speed, not more. The motorway traveller is often oblivious to the pace of things.

As we emerged blinking from beneath the bridge the panorama opened up again. We returned to a sunny day, and the tyre noise gradually receded into the background. As the canal continued its course we came across a red-brick pub adorned with hanging baskets, full of brightly coloured flowers. Yet I remained stuck in the contrast I had just experienced. My third and final pondering took me to the darkest place of all: "When you are on the motorway," I thought, "you miss all the best pubs!" Is it possible to travel at such speed that we don't have time to take in the willow as it brushes past us, or the moorhen as it nests? Is it possible that I could miss the best white wine, and the beauty of the young girl who serves it? Could I be travelling so fast to get to the pub of my dreams, that I fail to notice all the pubs I'm driving past? Suppose what I'm left with is the anticipation of a final destination, and no journey at all? Has the question of our lives become, "Are we there yet?"

Making connections

Jesus spent a lot of time speaking to people who lived directly off the land. He often used images familiar to them – of a farmer (sower) farming, or seed growing. Anyone who works with seed knows that the virtue of the farmer is patience. As Fr Denis McBride writes: "The sower knows that he has to wait; the process demands that he wait upon the weather, the working of the soil, the slow thrust of life, before he can see the fruit of his labour. There is a time of work, of waiting, of hazard, of slow emergence." There is a clue to living happily here and it is about the pace of things.

The motorway isn't evil. In many ways it is a good thing and a means for us to come together quickly. The motorway however possesses of itself a subtle illusion. A life lived at eighty miles an hour doesn't feel fast. You'll barely notice your life passing by. The fast lane is about destinations. The hard shoulder is about crises. There is little in between other than various rates of fast. Slow down and you'll suffer abuse, since a mind bent upon destinations rarely sees another human, only the car in front. This is where our road rage comes from. We forget we are human.

In our effort to reach our destination we can lose sight of the fact that most of our lives are lived getting there. The journey is what life is all about and so the pace of the journey and what we learn from it actually matters. When the canal and motorway converged I became acutely aware of my desire to live for Friday night, or the end of term, or my next vacation, or my retirement. These are all destinations. These are not where God lives.

The sower understands that sowing, waiting, and harvesting are all part of it. Part of the joy of eating is the hunger that precedes it. Part of the joy of success is the struggle to achieve it. There are no short cuts, quick fixes, or fast tracks to help us jump the queue. If we want to get the most from our lives we have got to learn to appreciate what it means to wait, and to slow down. The alternative is a fast journey to becoming lost to ourselves. As Blaise Pascal puts it, "By means of a diversion, a man can avoid his own company". Have you met yourself recently?

Conversation starters

- Is your life speeding up or slowing down?
- Can we lose the pleasure of the journey by concentrating on the destination?

Chapter 16

"Awesome" in Canada

*For this people's heart has grown dull, and their
ears are hard of hearing, and they have shut their
eyes; so that they might not look with their eyes,
and listen with their ears, and understand with
their heart and turn – and I would heal them.
But blessed are your eyes, for they see, and your
ears, for they hear. Truly I tell you, many prophets
and righteous people longed to see what you see,
but did not see it, and to hear what you hear, but
did not hear it.*

Matthew 13:15-17

It is always a privilege to be invited to speak at a conference, especially when it is in the province of Alberta in Canada. When I first went there someone listened to my presentation and told me I was "awesome". It was moving, to have someone tell you that you are awesome. Until you realise that in Canada everything is awesome. The coffee is awesome, the cookies are awesome, the weather is awesome, my accent is awesome, even the table decorations are awesome.

Several years ago I had an opportunity to take my family to see the Rocky Mountains. The Rockies are not easy to comprehend unless you have stood among them. The mountains stand tall and proud, vast beyond imagination, crowned in pure white snow and dressed at the lower levels by a thick carpet of deep green pine trees. Through this remarkable landscape a road known as Highway 93, the Icefields Parkway, wends its way around numerous mountain spurs. The road accompanies the great Athabasca River, which roars and plummets through carved white water gorges. There you are in the company of big shadows, crawling glaciers, spectacular waterfalls and what should surely be the world's most unnecessary sign advising visitors not to feed bears.

I'm driving along, my head pressed awkwardly against the windscreen, trying to look upwards without crashing into the campervan in front. It is impossible to contain my enthusiasm: "Just look at that mountain, that's Mount Robson." I'm explaining to my children that what we see is the highest mountain in the Rockies with glaciers running off it, but my geography lesson goes unheard. The children are arguing over a can of Coke – then comes the question: "Can we watch a video?" I'm driving along what is probably the most beautiful route in the world and they want to watch *Madagascar 2.* I'm exasperated. It was inconceivable to me that I would ever get to see these sights, and here we are wanting a cartoon on the in-car entertainment system. How on earth do we get the people we love to see what we can see, to see through our eyes?

In preparation for our trip we had explained where we were going, what we could do, and we showed the children a book with lots of pictures of the Rockies. We told them they could each choose an activity and showed them the sorts of options we could afford. Matthew was struck by a picture of a small boat with a tiny 50cc motor on the back. He wanted to go onto a lake in a small boat with a motor. That would be his treat.

Just above the town of Jasper is a kidney-shaped lake known as Pyramid Lake, named after the mountain that stands resplendent beside it. We would hire a motorboat there. It was early morning and no wind had yet stirred up the water. There was a perfect calm and serenity about it all. As the sun came up it caused the iron minerals in the mountains beyond to shine an orange and pink hue. Before our very eyes the pyramid mountain became a warm and inviting backdrop to the deep freshwater lake which lay before us like glass. The mountain, now glowing, was reflected upside down in the water. With perfect symmetry the pyramid was transformed into a diamond. To this day, it remains one of the most beautiful sights I have ever seen.

We pushed our little boat away from the jetty and headed out across the lake. With the water so idle and the image so perfectly reflected, it felt as though we were stepping into a painting. We stood in the flimsy boat, rocking from side to side, and I pointed towards the scene. The colour of the water was now unlike anything I had ever seen, even in a box of crayons, somewhere close to azure. There was silence and then I said to the boys: "Look, it is like falling into a picture, isn't it perfect?" In reply, Matthew gave me that look he gives me when he thinks I have asked him a stupid question, "What?" he said. He looked in the direction of my pointing finger, and then said again, "What?" The panorama, the mountain, the water, the sun's transforming light, he couldn't see what I was looking at. He looked confused and then said, "Yes Dad," simply wanting the question to go away. Then he went back to dragging his hand in the water as the boat made its way across to the other side.

Momentarily I was distracted by a memory of watching teenagers being coerced into walking up the hills close to where I lived in the Peak District. They couldn't see either. There would be a zealous dad with his trousers stuck inside his socks and his map in a plastic wallet. Several hundred metres behind would be two teenagers walking along with their knuckles almost dragging on the floor, hoping that at the top of the next hill would be a McDonald's and a games machine.

After looking for pirates and bear prints in the lake's shoreline, we headed back in the boat towards the jetty. The highlight for the children had been taking command of the small motor as captain of the ship. We'd had a happy morning. Matthew lay for a while at the bow of the boat, his hands draped over either side, his fingers cutting through the water as it moved. Then there was commotion, the boat rocking.

"Dad, Dad," said Matthew, beckoning me forward. "Dad," he said again, impatiently this time.

As I carefully made my way to the front, trying not to capsize us, I realised that whatever was exciting Matthew needed immediate attention. Sitting on his hand was the biggest dragonfly any of us had ever seen. It had taken refuge on him and, unaware of the attention it was attracting, proceeded to spread out its wings as if to dry them out.

Matthew has an eye for detail. Long after the others got bored with the sight he was still inspecting the creature. Counting its legs. It wouldn't be long before it had a name and he'd be talking to it.

"Dad," he said, staring with eyes wide open, "the colour on its back".

"Yes," I said, "what about the colour on its back?"

He paused as if to get the words right. "The colour on its back is the same as the colour of the water."

He silenced me. For once I shut up, realising that I had just been taught a lesson about looking at the world.

A week later I'm speaking at a conference in the nearby city of Edmonton. The people are generous in applause and present me with a small token of their appreciation. They told me I was "awesome". It was kind of them, but I wasn't awesome. "Awesome" is a dragonfly on the back of a child's hand.

Making connections

So many stories in the Gospels are about being able to see or hear things. These references shouldn't be taken literally. If we do that, it can give us the impression that only clever people see or hear things, in the same way that clever people quickly grasp quadratic equations or Chaucer. It was once my privilege to hear a deaf woman giving a talk about Jesus curing deafness and why the story had nothing to do with her ears and everything to do with her heart. To see or hear in the language of Jesus is not biological. In the Gospel stories Jesus links the ability to see and hear not with grasp, but with attitude. Are we open, enquiring, curious, hungry, humble enough to keep learning from him? Several times when teaching his disciples, Jesus criticises them – not for being stupid, although at times you begin to wonder – but because he is challenging the hardening of their hearts.

In every aspect of human endeavour, we want our children to see beauty wherever we see it. Whether instilling in our children total loyalty to our beloved football team, or an insistence on piano lessons. Whether our kids get it or not, we want them to view their lives the way we do ours. We can be heartbroken when they grow up and stop being like us. Whether it emerges as, "She won't come with me to church any more," or, "He's given up on his education," the grieving and loss of who we are inside of them is very painful. The difficult and painful realisation is that other people, including our children, are not versions of us.

The good news is that what I saw in the vast panorama, Matthew saw on the back of his hand. Our task is to show others how to look, God's task is to show them he's there. We can't do that bit. Matthew couldn't see the mountain's reflection, but he saw a reflection on a dragonfly's back. God will show himself to Matthew in his way, not mine. The most important thing I can do is show him that there is something worth looking for. Now that is Awesome!

Conversation starters

- Have you ever been able to see or appreciate what others seem unable to?
- Can what matters to us influence others, so that it matters to them?

Chapter 17

Learning how to remember

When the hour came, he took his place at the table, and the apostles with him. He said to them, "I have eagerly desired to eat this Passover with you before I suffer; for I tell you, I will not eat it until it is fulfilled in the kingdom of God." Then he took a cup, and after giving thanks he said, "Take this and divide it among yourselves; for I tell you that from now on I will not drink of the fruit of the vine until the kingdom of God comes." Then he took a loaf of bread, and when he had given thanks, he broke it and gave it to them, saying, "This is my body, which is given for you. Do this in remembrance of me." And he did the same with the cup after supper, saying, "This cup that is poured out for you is the new covenant in my blood."

Luke 22:14-20

A t 7.30 a.m. on the first of July 1916, the whistles blew along the trenches and the men ascended makeshift ladders to meet with their tragic destiny. Whether it was a hopeless plan, fumbled timing, or inevitable given the circumstances, the military gain was negligible and the losses were extreme. Timing was everything. The delay between the bombardment of the enemy trenches and the call to advance gave the German machine gunners enough time to reposition. The bombardment merely lifted, tangled and then dropped the barbed wire back into place. The men were cut to pieces as they stumbled through the shell holes, negotiated the wire and finally engaged with an enemy which was ready and waiting. A million men, mainly French and British soldiers, were killed or wounded in one of the most ambitious and catastrophic battles of the First World War.

Because the British government did not want people to witness thousands of bodies returning back to the British Isles, makeshift grave sites were quickly chosen and later adopted and redesigned by the War Graves Commission. These graveyards now serve as a marker for the line of trenches which once cut a swathe across the region of Picardy. There are many such grave sites and memorials around the French town of Albert – some vast, some with only a handful of graves. In the summer of 1996, with a small group of extended family, we travelled to the area known more infamously as the valley of the Somme.

On a hill between Albert and Bapaume stands the monument at Thiepval. Designed by Sir Edwin Lutyens, the monument of brick and stone stands forty-five metres high and can be seen for miles and miles. Sixteen pillars at its base provide enough stone panels for the names of 73,367 British and Commonwealth soldiers who died there in battle between July and November 1916.

It is impossible not to be struck by this place. Firstly, its scale is impressive. The monument swallows up its visitors, reflecting the enormity of what happened here. Secondly, its symmetry gives rise to a sense of order and formality. Nothing is an accident here. Sixteen pillars clustered into groups of four form the monument's legs. These are then united into two groups of eight and finally into an enormous arch which unites all the columns into one tower. There is no wasted space, no interruption to the lines in the design. It is a strong, solid, purposeful, unmistakable statement.

When we visit the monument, it is pristine. It has just rained. The stone slabs beneath us glisten in the sunshine. There is no litter, no untidiness or graffiti, nothing which would contradict the discipline of the memorial. People are walking slowly, standing still, speaking in hushed tones. Every name carved into the stone deserves as much. Every name on the panels tells a story of courage and fear: of loved ones back home weeping at the sight of the approaching postman, telegram in hand. A lost generation, inscribed upon these pillars, no grave to mark their lives. One can do little more than to stand still and be still.

Just a few miles from Thiepval near the village of Beaumont-Hamel is the Newfoundland Memorial. The site is owned by the Canadian government and is dedicated to the Newfoundland Regiment. On 1 July 1916, the battle was the regiment's first military engagement and it was almost entirely wiped out in the first thirty minutes of conflict. Three plaques there identify 814 Newfoundlanders for whom no known graves exist.

The memorial is a contrasting experience to the Thiepval monument. The seventy-four-acre site was largely the vision of Colonel Tom Nagle, a Roman Catholic priest in the regiment who soon after the war managed to negotiate with French landowners to buy the land. Known as the Newfoundland Memorial Park, the battle front upon which the regiment made its unsuccessful advance was left to stand much as it did on Armistice Day. The Newfoundland government made the decision to preserve a section of the battlefield, to leave it well alone as a memorial to their fallen, a park rather than a tower.

Today, tourists wander sunken paths in this strangely undulating landscape. Trees have grown since battle raged here, and the soil is now covered by a blanket of grass, but make no mistake, you are walking in shell holes and trenches – the setting for terrifying aggression and brutality. After a heavy thunderstorm, bullets and shell cases still surface in the washed-out soil. Short metal poles can be found here and there which once supported barbed wire. Most remarkably, you can walk a short distance and stand in the trenches which were once the makeshift home of the German soldiers. In doing so, you have just crossed a tiny patch of land which divided Europe, defined a generation, and was the bloody killing field of an entire battalion. The experience is chilling. To wander these trenches should be compulsory in anyone's growing up.

The experience of these two memorials was completely different, yet in each it was difficult not to be moved by the weight of the sacrifice. Both called into question the stupidity of this gargantuan war, and yet each place provided a unique testimony to courage, camaraderie, and ultimately willingness to lay down one's life for others. I resolved to write about it one day, because standing before thousands upon thousands of carved names or sitting in a hole whose existence probably brought about the end of someone's life made me realise that sacrifice above all things must be remembered. To forget it would be yet another disaster.

⚏ Making connections

When I was a little boy, my dad ran behind me holding the back of the saddle as I peddled my bike. It was not obvious the moment he let go. I was riding my bike without him and I didn't realise it. That lesson has lasted a lifetime. Learning to be a disciple isn't like learning to ride a bicycle. Most of the big lessons in life aren't like that. Strangely we forget the most important things, and so we have to learn them over and over again. I'm quite capable of forgetting what really matters. The skill therefore is to learn how to remember.

Our memory is one means by which we understand who we are. To lose our memory is tragic because our identity is lost with it. For some people, memories are best evoked inside a formal space. In a Catholic church for example, everything is ordered and occasionally reordered. The position and arrangement of things is deliberate. Nothing is casual or left to chance. There is a reason for everything being where it is. What happens there reflects that order. The pattern, repetition and formality allow people to encounter transcendence, to go beyond themselves and their own preoccupations. Through familiarity and order the Catholic enters into a sacred memorial. There is something similar about the Thiepval monument. Its order and formality make space for reverence. The carved names tell the story, and the structure of the monument indicates its purpose. The formality of the monument is a trigger for our collective memory.

To sit in a shell hole, on the other hand, is a way of remembering, but in a different way. Here the emphasis is on personal experience bringing to life a connection with what has happened. For some, the shell hole is more emotive and striking since it arrests the imagination and demands interpretation. Here you are left more to your own devices, scattered into seventy-four acres. The story is not carved out for you in stone panels. A trip into the undulating killing fields is a less regulated more informal experience, and the discovery more individual. The memorial park does not achieve what the monument can, but its impact can be as powerfully evocative.

Jesus gave us bread and wine as the means by which to remember him. He understood that we need to eat in order to live, and in eating we would be reminded of him daily. Eating is life-giving, a time of connection, of uniting, of intimacy with one another. We mark the most important moments of our lives with a meal. In choosing a meal as a means to remember, Jesus knew he would become part of our daily consciousness. What a wonderful understanding of how people remember.

Throughout my life I have met faithful people who will fall out with each other over how to remember. For some the place of remembering is a place of order, a setting for a sacred and mystical memorial. There are others who find the formality claustrophobic and remember God in a more personal context.

The greater gift is to learn how to remember in both spaces, in the temple and the desert, in the synagogue and the lonely place, at the altar and the kitchen table. The great mistake is to forsake one for the other.

Conversation starters

- What triggers our memories?
- How do shared rituals or experiences help us to remember together?

Chapter 18

Stupid me

You have heard that it was said, "You shall not commit adultery." But I say to you that everyone who looks at a woman with lust has already committed adultery with her in his heart. If your right eye causes you to sin, tear it out and throw it away; it is better for you to lose one of your members than for your whole body to be thrown into hell. And if your right hand causes you to sin, cut it off and throw it away; it is better for you to lose one of your members than for your whole body to go into hell.

Matthew 5:27-30

There are two versions of me. The first version thinks before he speaks, considers the implications of his actions, recognises the value of other people, acts justly, and loves without thought of gain. The second is worryingly stupid.

It is late in October and the weather forecast predicts the arrival of storm-force south-westerly winds. The town where I live is situated at the mouth of a narrow estuary. When the mighty waves are funnelled in from the Atlantic and, should they combine with a high tide, the effect is truly spectacular.

The town of Exmouth developed as a Victorian seaside town because of the coming of the railway and the erection of a grand concave sea wall. Built in 1842, the wall enabled the reclamation of the land behind and led to the construction of houses close up to the sea itself. For over a hundred and fifty years those limestone blocks have stood resolute against the battering of the relentless tides. The clever curve in the design enables the momentum of the rolling waves to be turned upwards. The waves hit the wall and as they do so become fountains of water propelled up high by their own energy. These lumbering waves which begin their journey many miles out to sea will finish it here abruptly, crashing onto the esplanade in Exmouth.

Gathering my children in the car we head to the seafront to view the ensuing spectacle. It is night and the ominous dark waters are caped with white windswept spray. Positioning ourselves carefully behind the wall we watch the sinister waves approach out of the darkness, lit by the streetlight behind us. The deep thump of the water as it hits the wall is followed by an almighty geyser shooting upwards and above us. Then this immense shower douses us all as it crashes onto the road. We laugh and splash and dance in the spray as it floods the street.

Cars parked precariously along the seafront sit in trapped seawater as wave upon wave pounds the wall with a regular rhythm. Other observers have arrived too, gathered in a nearby seafront shelter, screaming as tons of water fall upon the glass-and-timber structure. In this cold autumnal night, there is much childish joy in a place where sea and land converge, where nature's attack meets humankind's ingenious defence. We all marvel at this baptism of salt water.

We are cold now, and the prospect of warming drinks beckons us. Scooping the children up we return to the warmth of home. We shower, this time in warm controlled water, a trickle by comparison, and then wrap up in thick towels. Refreshed and exhilarated we relax content and tired after our adventure. Turning on the television we flick the channels to see if the local news has caught up with tonight's natural spectacle. After the dramatic opening music of the early evening news the first item announces: "After storms hit the south west local coast guards couldn't believe the stupidity of people who put themselves and others in danger

– emergency services are on high alert." Then there are televised scenes of people like us standing in the waves. We look at each other: "Stupid," I think, "have I just been stupid?"

The next day provides an answer. The morning brings one of those crisp, cold, bright autumn days. The strong winds have gifted us a clear day. The sky is a vivid royal blue, with the sea a similar colour. There are still some impressive waves but the tide is out and the beach is absorbing them all. In the bright light of a sunny day the sea is inviting. Even though it is cold, the colour of the water gives it its more regular appeal. There is nothing sinister or ruthless about its movement now.

But the clue to what just happened doesn't lie in the waters; it lies beneath our feet. As we walk along the esplanade the pavement is unrecognisable, covered in rocks and sea-borne debris. The cars parked there overnight have been dashed and scratched by what was lifted from the ocean floor. Pebbles and boulders are strewn across the road and piled up against houses. People who live near the sea understand its capacity to carry a quarry-load of debris and dump it onto tidy spaces. Aware of the capacity of a swollen sea to drag victims into the water I had been careful where I stood with the children. What I failed to understand was that the water falling upon our heads could so easily have deposited a boulder on any one of us. Growing up far from the sea I was having to learn what is so obvious to those who live near it. Had I been stupid? Once again the answer was a resounding yes!

⚮ Making connections

What ever happened to sin? Sin used to be understood as shameful and embarrassing but today it seems almost the opposite. Sin is so synonymous with pleasure that luxury items market themselves as sins, assuming it will make the product attractive. This loss of a sense of sin has not been good for us.

As a boy I would be taken to confession. To confess my sins to a priest I had first to understand what sin was. Catholic teaching defines sin as an offence against "reason, truth and right conscience" and tells us that "Sin sets itself against God's love for us" *(Catechism of the Catholic Church, 1850).* These definitions are hard for small children and so in order to help a tiny mind understand, the teacher would offer examples, lots of them. They included such things as being disobedient to parents, not paying attention at Mass, or arguing with brothers and sisters. These examples were to teach us to cultivate a sense of our own wrongdoing. The problem though, was that at seven years old I didn't feel especially wrong about the things I was confessing. At times I found myself making up sins to please the confessor. It seems that on reflection I was lying in the confessional. If I hit my brother, it was because I thought that he deserved it.

If our understanding of sin matures from a child's version it can become helpful. In AD 590 Pope Gregory gave us seven deadly sins: gluttony, avarice, sloth, wrath, envy, pride and lust. When I look at this list I see seven gradual means by which to self-destruct. In each one I see what St Paul calls an "illusory desire" that ultimately leads to people hating themselves and damaging others. If God is offended by our sin it is because he wants us to be happy. We need a healthy sense of what compromises our happiness. The Church calls that sin. Being taught about sin wasn't meant to lead to a life of guilt-induced shame.

In Matthew's Gospel we read this graphic call to rip out an eye if it causes us to sin. People who take the Bible literally rarely quote this verse. The strength of the imagery is there to help us recognise the risks attached to what we desire. Not everything we want is good for us. Any addict will tell you about being consumed by a desire to the detriment of everything else in their lives.

Inside me I know there is a stupid me. Stupid me takes himself too seriously, obsesses about his own reputation, is consumed by pointless anxiety, feels threatened by other people's success, works too hard, eats too much, and imagines himself to be important. A healthy sense of sin reminds me that to act on any of these stupid impulses will lead to certain self-loathing. Being a disciple doesn't kill off stupid me, and neither does stupid me stop being persuasive. I go to church because I'm sinful and stupid, not because I've stopped being like that.

Stupid me didn't set out to hurt my children in the seawater spray. Stupidity comes from a mixture of ignorance and desire. Like so much stupidity we recognise the real sin only after the event, when the damage is done. There are all sorts of debris in our lives. The important thing is to recognise it, name it, own up to it, and start learning to avoid it. I try to be a good man, but there is a mad, sad, stupid me and every now and again he escapes.

Conversation starters

- Has society lost a sense of sin?
- Is it healthy to have a sense of sin?

Chapter 19

Looking for Trafalgar Square

When the Son of Man comes in his glory, and all the angels with him, then he will sit on the throne of his glory. All the nations will be gathered before him, and he will separate people one from another as a shepherd separates the sheep from the goats, and he will put the sheep at his right hand and the goats at the left. Then the king will say to those at his right hand, "Come, you that are blessed by my Father, inherit the kingdom prepared for you from the foundation of the world; for I was hungry and you gave me food, I was thirsty and you gave me something to drink, I was a stranger and you welcomed me, I was naked and you gave me clothing, I was sick and you took care of me, I was in prison and you visited me." Then the righteous will answer him, "Lord, when was it that we saw you hungry and gave you food, or thirsty and gave you something to drink? And when was it that we saw you a stranger and welcomed you, or naked and gave you clothing? And when was it that we saw you sick or in prison and visited you?" And the king will answer them, "Truly I tell you, just as you did it to one of the least of these who are members of my family, you did it to me."

Matthew 25:31-40

There is something really stimulating about London. Whenever I get off the train, especially in iconic stations like St Pancras or Waterloo, I am wide eyed like a child. It would be different if I did this every day, but because I visit the metropolis only occasionally, it never fails to impress me. The excitement might remind me of my childhood visits here. The first time I got off a train at St Pancras station I was captivated by the size of the clock which hangs high up in the terminus. I spent the whole day walking the streets gawping upwards and around me at the buildings. Nowadays the stimulus is other things. Perhaps it's the anonymity you can experience in crowded places, or it might be the sheer diversity of the people and languages. Maybe it's the longevity of this city, so much older than all its inhabitants. Whatever it is, the big city is a testimony to human ingenuity. There's something thrilling about being part of it.

Amongst the deluge of colours, sounds and smells in London, the human can enter into strangely inhuman environments. It's not natural to be squeezed face to face in a labyrinth of underground tunnels like sardines in a can. Standing in a crowded tube train at rush hour can be miserable. It's hot, sweaty and impersonal. Despite standing in such tight proximity millions of us agree to avoid each other. Without it being a rule or law, no one speaks unless they know the person they're travelling with. There's no eye contact, no recognition, we move around each other with resolute skill without really encountering each other. As the train accelerates and the billboard advertisements blend into one another, an entire carriage settles into unwritten protocols. In such a crowded space, we are happily existing in completely isolated and separate worlds.

As the doors slide shut and we accelerate into another tunnel, heads tilt into opened books, newspapers are lifted to conceal faces, those left standing look to the floor. Everything is just as it should be. Until, from only a few feet away, a loud voice breaks into our private journeys. He is shouting to be heard above the repetitive clanking of the train's motion. There's nothing striking about this man except his insistence to speak to the entire carriage. He holds onto the safety bar with one hand and holds up a small black book with the other. "Ladies and gentleman," he begins, "I am here to tell you about the Lord Jesus Christ." His announcement continues with some mention of sin, and then a prediction about our eternal destiny if we don't turn to God. His message is delivered seriously, as a warning for us all. Without God we are in peril. We are in danger. He slaps his book as if it is each one of us.

His initial impact is that people in the carriage start to make eye contact. His transgression of the protocols is allowing people to recognise each other. All sorts of glances are now passing between us. The man opposite me lowers his paper and glances at our preacher. He takes the hand of the woman next to him to reassure her. Only now do I realise they are together. The woman standing next to me is carrying a map of London. She is sniggering and looking at the woman next to her; she whispers something in Spanish and they laugh. A small boy looks to his mum for confirmation that the situation is under control. She returns his anxious look with a mother's smile. Her expression tells him that all is well, and he goes back to the plastic puzzle he is intently playing with.

My awareness switches back to our preacher. I'm struck by his self-confidence and by the certainty with which he goes about his task. There is something admirable about his zeal, yet at the same time I'm also embarrassed by him. While I might share some of his convictions, I'm uncomfortable about his strategy. Is this what being a disciple is all about? Is he right to be doing this? Should I be in awe of him or irritated by him? Perhaps I am merely excusing my own timidity?

The train stops with its usual jolt, the doors slide open and everyone in our tiny compartment moves. Some people are weaving their way out of the carriage, replaced by new passengers with shopping bags. As the doors slide shut our preacher is gone. His absence returns us to our conventional ways. It all seems very quiet now. The man's newspaper is back up in front of his face and his wife is attending to her nails. Once again people are lost to each other.

The Spanish girls are still looking at their map in the carriage next to me. We had made brief eye contact during the speech.

"Excuse me, sir," says one of them politely, "there's no station called Trafalgar Square; what station is nearest to Trafalgar Square?" We have established contact. There is a brief moment of humanity in our carriage. Perhaps our preacher did achieve something after all.

👥 Making connections

The scene in the train carriage troubled me. As a disciple am I supposed to imitate the preacher? Is a disciple someone who disturbs commuters and carries on speaking regardless of his impact? The people around me seemed more irritated than challenged by his message. My reaction was to want him to disappear. Which he promptly did. At the next station.

At the end of our church service the priest or deacon sends us away with one of several written commissions. One of these states, "Go and announce the Gospel of the Lord," and another, "Go in peace, glorifying the Lord with your life." Most people only hear the word "Go". The difference between these two statements is important. While both send people away, one emphasises our commitment to speak of what we believe, while the other prioritises the way our lives demonstrate our words. Our ability to reach out effectively comes from both of these commissions.

On reflection two things were disconcerting about what I witnessed on the tube train. Firstly the preacher didn't know us; the man behind the newspaper and his wife, the Spanish tourists, the woman looking after her child remained strangers to him. His was not the harder task of building relationships, which demands so much more than shouting at people. This was not feeding the hungry or thirsty, welcoming strangers, caring for the sick, or building relationships with prisoners which we read of in Matthew 25. His lack of relationship with us was hindering his ability to connect meaningfully with his audience. As if consumed by the importance of what he had to say, he ignored the carriage of people. The people responded in kind. The avoidance became mutual. If anything, he drew people together in their fleeting glances, but his words were not at the heart of it.

Secondly and more importantly, when the doors closed we could not walk away. The preacher chose a confined space for a reason. It hadn't struck me before but the greatest teachers don't coerce their students. Christianity by its very nature cannot be forced onto people. Preaching shouldn't be fuelled by anxiety. The Christian message should never bully or intimidate, which is why at baptism we begin with a question: "What do you ask of God's Church?" The answer has to be freely given without coercion before the sacrament can be administered.

It wasn't that he got on the train that irritated me most, although his speech didn't work for me. Perhaps for one or two people his message may have been timely. The problem for me was that he got off it. For his message to be understood he needed to be prepared to enter into the journey of the people he was shouting at. With such courage he should have been able to listen to their response and face their indignation. Perhaps next time he might make more of a difference if he was prepared to go out of his way for someone, and show them the way to Trafalgar Square.

Conversation starters

- Do street preachers and door-to-door evangelists deserve our admiration or irritation?
- Are we more persuaded by a message or by a person's behaviour?

Chapter 20

Surprised by joy

Jesus knew that they wanted to ask him, so he said to them, "Are you discussing among yourselves what I meant when I said, 'A little while, and you will no longer see me, and again a little while, and you will see me'? Very truly, I tell you, you will weep and mourn, but the world will rejoice; you will have pain, but your pain will turn into joy. When a woman is in labour, she has pain, because her hour has come. But when her child is born, she no longer remembers the anguish because of the joy of having brought a human being into the world. So you have pain now; but I will see you again, and your hearts will rejoice, and no one will take your joy from you. On that day you will ask nothing of me. Very truly, I tell you, if you ask anything of the Father in my name, he will give it to you. Until now you have not asked for anything in my name. Ask and you will receive, so that your joy may be complete."

John 16:19-24

Writing a "bucket list" has become a popular way to describe what we want to achieve before we die. The same sort of things frequently feature high on these lists. They generally fall into broader categories such as travelling to exotic places, various acts of daring and getting closer to nature. More specifically, visiting the Great Wall of China, bungee jumping and scuba-diving with turtles.

In the top five of most bucket lists you'll usually find swimming with dolphins. For some reason which I don't quite understand, lots of us want to swim with large smiley-faced fish-like mammals before we die. All sorts of attributes have been attached to the experience of swimming with dolphins. They are attributed with the power to release people from stress and boredom and have even been associated with healing from physical or mental illness. Swimming with dolphins must be a rewarding experience and thoroughly enjoyable, but is it really the best we can come up with? Riding an elephant in Thailand features highly too. There must be something within us that longs to interact with nature's greatest celebrities. Dolphins and elephants clearly make something happen for us that your local donkey ride can't.

Having an adrenalin rush features high on bucket lists too: abseiling off a high building, parachuting, cliff jumping, white-water rafting. A number of times I have put myself into situations which cause me to doubt my own sanity. As a teacher I was given an opportunity to learn to ski with the pupils I taught. The first time an instructor told us to ski in a straight line down a glacial slope I remember going so fast that I thought I was going to die. "I'm going to die, I'm going to die," I repeated to myself out loud over and over. The experience of not dying was exhilarating. With one act of daring I was hooked to the idea of putting fibreglass planks onto my feet and falling forwards down a mountain. Thanks to that opportunity, skiing has continued to thrill me all my life.

There are so many ways to feel truly accomplished. So many things to achieve before we die. But something about these things and their impact on us changes through life. After a conference in Los Angeles my hosts took me to Disneyland as a treat. This theme park, the very first of its kind, personifies how America plays. It's innovative, vibrant and extravagant. It is hard not to be drawn into the magic of it all. Music is playing everywhere, cartoon characters appear out of nowhere for photo opportunities and there's nothing to tarnish this surreal playground. It was lovely to be with these people in what claims to be the "happiest place on earth".

Because our group was made up of an odd number, as we queued to get on a rollercoaster I found myself alone in a carriage. This million-dollar high-tech ride propelled me through huge drops and tight loops. Pinned to my seat by the G-force I realised I wasn't laughing. Normally I'd shout and laugh nervously through this kind of ride. Strangely, despite the extreme circumstance, I found myself feeling homesick. The ride wasn't working without my teenage children who would love this moment. It was as if I didn't know how to enjoy the rollercoaster without them. It isn't clear to me just when it happened, but I had moved on. Not by any virtue of my own, my bucket list couldn't be about just me any more.

I'm sitting in the lounge at home. It is a typical November evening, dark and damp outside. A fire warming us, a television half entertaining us, drawn curtains keeping the winter outside. Alison is curled up on the sofa lost in her book. Sam is playing a game on the computer, campaigning for world domination. Matt and Emily are arguing over the remote control for the television. I'm sitting there among them, unengaged by the television and wondering how to motivate myself to do something more productive. There is nothing extraordinary about any of this. It is just a Tuesday night at home in November.

What happens next is hard to describe. It is a moment of grace that I haven't conjured or deserved. Unannounced, I'm visited by a deep sense of joy. Why this joy has fallen upon me I have no idea, I am taken by surprise by it. It transforms a mundane scene into something meaningful. It's as though I'm looking at my life through different eyes. While I can't hear any words, what I can feel happening is a revelation to this effect: "David, this is as good as your life gets. If you don't see it now, you never will." I have an overwhelming sense of gratitude for the scene I'm looking at and it moves me to tears. My family are together, I think, and we are safe and alive. With the joy comes a tremendous sense of appreciation for what I already have. All I can do is say, "Thank you", which I do. No one else is aware of this personal epiphany.

Strange as it seems, this awareness left me just as quickly as it arrived. No sooner did I sense it, than it had gone. Stranger still, I didn't try to hold on to it or hanker for it. I'd been given the gift to see briefly my life as it truly is, a thing of great beauty. It was enough to know it, even for a short while. This joy was not the product of wild bursts of adventure, the eye-opening travel opportunities I enjoy, or the possibility of one day swimming with turtles. It was a deeper joy, and it made me grateful for a mundane Tuesday evening in November.

Making connections

Joy is often confused with laughter, happiness, pleasure and achievement. These may be symptoms of its presence, but of themselves they are not joy. For some people the presence of joy brings tears and silence rather than laughter and celebration. Anyone who has experienced joy will tell you that it emerges from deep within us rather than in the circumstances around us. You can't purchase it, manufacture it, conjure it, contrive it or expect it. If that were the case, the rich would be noticeably more joyful than the poor and it is obvious that they are not. The author C. S. Lewis encountered it as unexpected and unrequested "stabs" in his life, hence his reference to William Wordsworth's poem, "Surprised by joy – impatient as the wind".

John's Gospel contains numerous references to joy. In this passage Jesus promises joy after a time of suffering. It is not that joy is promised instead of suffering, which most people naturally pray for, or that it will be offered as a reward for suffering. It is as if emerging out of our pain is an almost unexpected encounter with a deeper joy. Here, joy comes after longing, striving, struggling.

This relationship between joy and longing is worthy of reflection. Joy visits us by grace rather than through merit, often when we least expect it. It causes the heart to swell, it diminishes the attention we afford to our own suffering, it gives rise to a sense of gratitude for what we already have and it causes us to realign our priorities. All these things can bring us deep contentment.

In John's Gospel joy happens when the human encounters the divine. This is what Pope Francis means when he refers to "the joy of the Gospel" ("The Joy of the Gospel"). Joy is what happens when people encounter Jesus. In Jesus' impending return, joy will no longer be fleeting, it will be permanent. Heaven will be joy in residence.

Humanity is ingenious. It can throw itself from aeroplanes and live, it can put flags on the highest mountains or observe the behaviour of the world's most endangered species. These things are wonderful. They are, though, their own reward. Joy on the other hand is not a possession of the privileged or the most dedicated. Joy is a gift, and those who have encountered it know that it is beyond our efforts to achieve it. Perhaps a fulfilled life includes an encounter with joy. Now that is worthy of a place on anyone's bucket list.

Conversation starters

- When people speak about joy, what do they mean?
- Is a feeling of personal achievement different to the joy religious people speak of?

Chapter 21

Taking his place

He sternly ordered and commanded them not to tell anyone, saying, "The Son of Man must undergo great suffering, and be rejected by the elders, chief priests, and scribes, and be killed, and on the third day be raised." Then he said to them all, "If any want to become my followers, let them deny themselves and take up their cross daily and follow me. For those who want to save their life will lose it, and those who lose their life for my sake will save it. What does it profit them if they gain the whole world, but lose or forfeit themselves? Those who are ashamed of me and of my words, of them the Son of Man will be ashamed when he comes in his glory and the glory of the Father and of the holy angels."

Luke 9:21-26

There is something quite mysterious about teaching teenagers. The conundrum is to do with watching an eleven-year-old morph into an eighteen-year-old. In just seven years a child becomes a young adult, and if you're fortunate to be taken into their trust it is a privilege to be there. As a new cohort of timid fresh-faced newcomers arrive, you can't really be sure what sort of people are about to emerge before your eyes. In my teaching career I met many remarkable young people. Occasionally someone extraordinary sits in your classroom, who in the course of their time in school will teach you far more than you'll ever teach them. A joy of teaching is that when they first arrive it is impossible to know who that will be.

In the first few years you could be forgiven for barely noticing Sally. She required little in the way of help and unlike so many teenagers rarely sought attention. Through her early teens she worked really hard and was eager to please. She enjoyed the company of a small group of girls, succeeded in just about everything she tried, and appeared to be growing into a genuinely happy young person. By the time she was fourteen she was displaying a strong academic ability and achieving top grades. What was equally pleasing was that the other students liked her. During one parents' evening I remember saying to her mum and dad that if I had a daughter I'd want her to be like Sally. I meant it. Sally loved life, loved learning and loved people; she was for all these reasons delightful to have in the classroom.

The news came to me from her form teacher. Sally would not be in school for a while. In a tragic accident her younger brother who was not yet old enough to be in our school had died. As her religious studies teacher I did not want to make sense of this tragedy or come out with platitudes about heaven. My instinct was just to recognise Sally's pain and to be available if she needed me. She didn't. She was part of a remarkably loving family who gathered in close confines and bore their pain in privacy. They suffered with remarkable dignity away from any public attention. They would face their trauma together.

Events like this strangely bring out the best in a community. For a while a sort of peace broke out in the school, as concern for Sally affected everyone. Arguments about budgets and rotas were briefly put into perspective by the loss of a young life. Within a short time Sally was back among us, having chosen to carry on with the normal things of life.

Many of my lessons involved discussion so it was not unusual for the students to talk about their beliefs. On several occasions the following year Sally chose to speak openly about her suffering and how her faith had helped. Listening to her I felt unqualified to teach her anything. Her faith and courage were carrying her through a darkness the rest of us couldn't imagine. During a conversation about prayer she spoke gently about the night her brother died and when she finished speaking there was silence. Not the sort of silence you call for, but a silence of respect. It is rare to see thirty teenagers speechless. Although many of these young people didn't go anywhere near a church, they knew as I did that we were sharing a privileged moment, hearing something authentic, something you don't learn from a book. Unintentionally and unconsciously she was doing the real teaching. On such rare occasions the skill of the teacher is to learn to get out of the way.

Six months later it is time for a final parents' evening. There is the usual mix of anxious parents, curious parents, a few "I give up" parents, all anticipating the run-in towards final public examinations. As I'm speaking to an anxious mother about the future prospects of her son, I notice that next in line, sitting patiently, are Sally's mum and dad. As the mother stands up to shake my hand I'm aware that I haven't seen them since their tragedy. Having not grieved myself I'm suddenly at a loss. Do I mention their loss? Do I ignore it? Do we carry on as if nothing has happened? What is the right thing to do in moments like this? There is no manual, no convention, no protocol.

There's no need to be anxious. Sally's parents come to my desk and greet me warmly. Quickly putting me at ease Sally's dad tells me, "Sally loves your lessons." "I love teaching her," I reply immediately, and we begin by talking about what a gifted student Sally is. My finger is running along the list of her assignment grades, "Is she thinking of university?" I ask. "These grades are outstanding." We discuss her future plans and time is quickly running out. Another family is waiting in line. I'm disappointed in myself. We have talked easily about her ability but I have not spoken of her courage.

Sally's parents stand up and shake my hand enthusiastically. My mind is racing. The thought of not mentioning their trauma seems unforgivable. As they are about to turn away the words come out of my mouth before I've thought them through: "It must have been hard," I offer pathetically, "and... I'm sorry," I add. It seems awkward and forced but better than saying nothing at all.

Sally's mother looks at me as though I've done the right thing. Her eyes betray long nights of suffering. There have been many tears on that face which has now broken into a generous smile. She looks across to her husband as if to await his reply. Sally's dad looks intently at me for a second, "Mr Wells," he says, "there hasn't been a day go by where I wouldn't have taken the boy's place," and in a final gesture, as if to offer a little reassurance, he adds, "but, we'll be okay." As they walk away it becomes easy to understand why Sally is so strong. Love like this will endure all things, even the loss of an only son.

Making connections

In this passage Jesus declares that he will suffer rejection and death and then, somewhat worryingly for us, ask his followers to do likewise. The job prospects don't look too promising. It doesn't look like we are heading for a relaxed retirement on good benefits. We are asked to take up a cross, follow him towards death, and ultimately to give up our lives. Who would want to do that? Surely Jesus is going to lose followers with this stipulation.

The command looks too hard for us unless we understand this passage in the context of love. One of the most beautiful and unique aspects of our humanity is our readiness to suffer for each other. We are willing to take on the burdens of another because we love them. We can find examples of it everywhere, in the parents of disabled children, in the man who chooses priesthood over a lucrative career, in countless stories in every street of people who give their lives to each other, for better and for worse. This sort of love which has no thought of self-advantage is, we discover, the greatest expression of love: "No one has greater love than this, to lay down one's life for one's friends" (John 15:13).

Suppose God wanted to demonstrate not power, authority or control, but love, complete and perfect love. How might he show it? Jesus goes before his Father and offers his life for ours. When Sally's dad told me that he would willingly have taken the boy's place I am in the presence of that same kind of sacrificial love. Through this man's love for his son, I was given a glimpse of how God looks at each one of us.

When called upon to lay down our lives in the service of others we are learning to love like God does.

Conversation starters

- Does all true love involve sacrifice?
- How do we respond to a belief that God suffered on our behalf?

Chapter 22

The coat of no arms

*A leper came to him begging him, and kneeling
he said to him, "If you choose, you can make me
clean." Moved with pity, Jesus stretched out his
hand and touched him, and said to him, "I do
choose. Be made clean!" Immediately the leprosy
left him, and he was made clean. After sternly
warning him he sent him away at once, saying
to him, "See that you say nothing to anyone;
but go, show yourself to the priest, and offer for
your cleansing what Moses commanded, as a
testimony to them." But he went out and began
to proclaim it freely, and to spread the word, so
that Jesus could no longer go into a town openly,
but stayed out in the country; and people came
to him from every quarter.*

Mark 1:40-45

We followed the river along a narrow winding
woodland trail. The sunny day was obscured by the
lush canopy of leaves above our heads. Occasionally,
bright columns of sunlight would pierce their way through and
light up the decaying forest carpet beneath us. It was with some
trepidation that we approached the trapeze. The trapeze, I was
told by the children, was the scariest dare of the week. Having
climbed, abseiled, zip-wired and flung myself around a variety of
obstacles trusting in harnesses and karabiner hooks, I was

beginning to get the hang of not falling. "It will be fine," I reassured myself. "If ten-year-olds can do it, I can."

To cheer us towards our impending challenge, we were prompted to sing "repeat after me" songs. The spirit in the camp was good. It was wonderful to have this opportunity. Each year a few parents from my children's school would volunteer to accompany the teachers on a residential activity week. Having missed so many evenings and weekends through my work, I saw it as an opportunity to make up for a little lost time.

The path now brought us to a glade in the woods with a tall post standing resolute in the middle surrounded by a circle of benches. Leaning against the post was a ladder. Sitting the class on benches our instructor began, "I'm looking for a volunteer," he said. "Someone big." It was obvious where this was going. "You, sir," he said beckoning me forward, "perhaps you would go first and demonstrate to all these lovely children just how safe the trapeze is." "Great," I thought, "now my trepidation is on trial."

Harnessed to a cable I begin my ascent up the ladder which brings me halfway up the post. I continue the climb supported by small footholds in the post. Our leader hasn't explained that the post will wobble, which makes it all very precarious. Having done a few things like this before, I know the trick is to act quickly. Think too much and reason will steal your courage, so I move as quickly as I can. At the top of the post sits a platform the size of a typical garden bird table. "Okay," says the instructor, "climb onto the platform and stand upright."

Despite the simplicity of the instruction, the task is surprisingly challenging. The platform is just big enough to stand on, but there's nothing to hold onto. My legs feel weak as I rise from my knees to a standing position. I'm aware of the small faces of children way down below me, my son included. Their gaze is fixed intently on my expression. The post wobbles vigorously. This is not the time to cry.

It is only now, my legs buckling, that I see some distance away a trapeze swaying gently in the breeze. "All you have to do is leap off and reach out for that trapeze," says a voice from the floor. "Is that all?" I think. It's no good telling myself it's safe, this is going to be a leap of faith, not of reason. "Just do it," I tell myself, and my weak legs push away. Clasping that trapeze turns out to be more rewarding than I expected. As I'm lowered safely to the ground by the harness, the endorphins in my brain are having a party. I'm still alive.

I was back at camp two years later with my second son. "You'll love the trapeze," I said, "it will be one of the highlights of the week." Matthew loved this sort of challenge. It would be my privilege to share it with him and his classmates as I had done with his older brother.

It was lunchtime, shortly before the trapeze session, when one of the boys rushed into the dining hall. "Please Miss," he said, breathless, to his teacher, "Matt's had an accident." The poor boy had reached for his wallet through the bars on his bunk bed and lost his footing on the bed below. As his body fell his arm was trapped and he heard his bone break. Despite taking part in a week of physical challenges, my son had managed to break his arm on his dormitory bed. As we drove back from the hospital that afternoon, his arm plastered from his elbow to his fingers, the look of disappointment was indelible. "Does it hurt?" I asked. "Not much," he said. He didn't want it to hurt. He wanted it to go away.

It seemed only right to explain that we could go back to the camp or go home. The choice was his. "I'm not going to get to do the trapeze am I?" he asked. It wasn't the thought of six weeks in a plaster-cast that bothered him so much as missing out on the activities. "If we go back it will be hard," I said to him. "Your friends will want to tell you all about the activities and they won't realise that you'll feel jealous." Considering the obvious disappointment, he made his decision: "Let's go back to the camp," he said, "I want to stay with my friends."

There is something about being a parent that breaks your heart. In the order of things a broken arm on a school trip is hardly a tragedy. Far worse things happen to other families. Yet here I was feeling disappointed for him. He'd looked forward to the trip ever since his brother had told him about it. All he could do now was watch.

As we arrived in the car park the class gathered around, keen to see his arm in plaster. At the age of ten there's something quite heroic about broken bones. "Off you go," I said, "I'll see you later." As I walked away I noticed the boys resuming a football game and Matt standing on the sidelines, his arm concealed inside his sweatshirt, an empty sleeve limp down by his side. During the short walk to the staff room to rejoin the other adults I found myself praying, "Lord, help him not to feel left out."

In the staff room we were talking about local hospitals, the state of our National Health Service, the speed at which bones heal, how wonderful nurses are, and Matthew's decision to return to the camp. "Dave," said one of the teachers, not listening to our conversation, "I think you should see this." Having explained how Matt's real injury was the thought of missing out, I stood up and joined her at the window. The two of us looked out across the playground to where the children were playing. There were boys, lots of them, all running around on a football pitch with their arms tucked up inside their jumpers, their empty sleeves flapping about in the evening sunshine. Matt among them. Every now and again, despite the cruelty and unkindness we dread, goodness triumphs. Sometimes even children can show us how the world should be.

Making connections

The cure of this leper features in three Gospels. In Mark's Gospel it features in the first chapter. Mark is using this miracle to quickly establish the essential and unique nature of Jesus' ministry. Jesus wants to restore the leper into human contact by healing him, and then into the religious community by referring him, as the law requires, to the priest. It is about restoring, reuniting and reconciling people. Jesus will come to the aid of the outcast, not just for the sake of marginalised, but for the building up of the entire community. In this way Jesus will restore one to the other and both will be healed.

There is a cost though. In two of the accounts of this incident, Jesus forgoes his own freedom. The cured man's enthusiasm makes Jesus suffer like a celebrity and the crowds prevent him from moving about freely. In a sense Jesus becomes the outcast, preferring the lonely places to the attention he attracts in the towns.

Occasionally you will see something similar in our efforts to love each other. Sometimes we recognise the isolation of others, seek to restore them, and pay a price in doing so. Sometimes the price is great, sometimes it is less so. This imitation of Christ strikes at the heart of discipleship. In identifying with Matthew's predicament, his classmates did something remarkable. They made his broken arm something which united them. They healed a division.

Sometimes you don't have to look to the mountains to see the hallmark of the Almighty. Sometimes you'll see it in the playground, among a handful of children doing their best to look after each other.

Conversation starters

- Where do we notice people being isolated or excluded?
- What are the challenges of helping people to integrate or join in?

Chapter 23

Are you keeping busy?

Jesus replied, "A man was going down from Jerusalem to Jericho, and fell into the hands of robbers, who stripped him, beat him, and went away, leaving him half dead. Now by chance a priest was going down that road; and when he saw him, he passed by on the other side. So likewise a Levite, when he came to the place and saw him, passed by on the other side. But a Samaritan while travelling came near him; and when he saw him, he was moved with pity. He went to him and bandaged his wounds, having poured oil and wine on them. Then he put him on his own animal, brought him to an inn, and took care of him. The next day he took out two denarii, gave them to the innkeeper, and said, 'Take care of him; and when I come back, I will repay you whatever more you spend.' Which of these three, do you think, was a neighbour to the man who fell into the hands of the robbers?" He said, "The one who showed him mercy." Jesus said to him, "Go and do likewise."

Luke 10:30-37

It was time to head back to our hotel on the outskirts of Berlin. The queue for the bus was building up and a large number of commuters had gathered. As it arrived we all edged forwards, anxious not to have to wait for a later bus. In scenes familiar in every city around the world, we were squeezing ourselves into a tight space in order to get home. Almost upon the platform at the front of the bus, a woman raised her hand and began to instruct the other commuters, "Excuse me," she said loudly and pointing, "could you move down the bus please?" A few passengers politely followed her instructions. Moving forward onto the bus the woman was more visible, and she continued with a more assertive request, "Do you mind moving towards the back and then a few more people down here can get onto the bus?" People were remarkably amenable and soon more passengers were filing onto the bus, including me.

The woman's confidence impressed me. She was shouting her instructions in English. I wondered what Londoners would make of a foreigner shouting instructions in German? As the bus progressed along its route the passengers disembarked and seats became available. As we reached the outer suburbs I found myself taking up a vacated space next to her. "Thank you," I said, "your request got me onto the bus." She smiled. "Crazy isn't it?" she said, "There's lots more room if everyone moves down the bus." "You're a teacher aren't you?" I said. She looked shocked as if I had been inside her head. "How did you know?" she said. I couldn't believe she was asking me.

While looking one day at an assortment of novelty gifts in a shop window in Devon, I saw a woman point at a mask of Tutankhamun and heard her say to her husband, "Oh, that would be good for the Egyptians." Here was another teacher giving her profession away while on holiday.

It is hard to switch off from being the job that we do. One evening at a works party, a colleague informed me that her husband was retiring later that year. Imagining it to be the right thing to say, I replied, "Oh that's wonderful. You must be looking forward to spending more time together." She looked at me as if I was stupid: "It isn't wonderful at all," she said indignantly. Seeing the look of perplexity on my face she added, "What on earth am I going to do with him?" We all laughed. We were acknowledging that any marriage that survives this long somehow arrives at that question. It made me wonder if we lose sight of who we are without our jobs. Now, almost like a stranger he's moving back into her life and her territory, but this time he's jobless. Almost as if he was a new piece of furniture, she was going to have to work out where to put him. I couldn't help but wonder if the harder we work, the more out of place we look when it's time to come home for good.

When we first moved to our present home we knew we would have to make an extra effort to meet people. The local pub, the neighbourhood, the parish, the school gate all presented opportunities for friendly conversation. No matter where we went the first conversation was almost invariably about employment. The question I was asked most often was usually this: "Well, David, what do you do?" Explaining that I work for a Roman Catholic diocese promoting adult education wasn't exactly a crowd pleaser. It wasn't easy making the job sound exotic and the conversation usually moved quickly on. Similarly when I first started teaching it was possible to empty an entire party with the answer, "I'm a religious studies teacher." Usually the only person to stick around to hear more was the person with unresolved religious vitriol, who would then proceed to lecture me about the hypocrisy of religion or his overbearing religious parents.

"What do you do?" became an exhausted question. I enjoy talking about work, but not too early on in a new friendship. In answer to the question I would mischievously come up with something like this, "Well, sometimes when I'm in the house on my own, I dance naked!" Then I'd add, "What do you do?" Almost invariably the conversation which followed was more animated than explaining my job to people who wish they hadn't asked.

While on a visit to Nigeria, I noticed that the questions people ask are different. Some were curious about my work of course, but there were many more questions about my family, my church, my children's school, my football team, my philosophy and life in general. "Tell me, David," said one man, "is it true that in England if I visit your house and you are reading your paper, you'd carry on reading your paper?" Where did that question come from? What had he been told about England? What a wonderful conversation starter.

Over time I noticed that, as well as having one preferred question, "What do you do?", we also have one preferred answer. Wherever I went the correct answer seemed to be, "Well, I'm very busy." In fact I noticed that social convention demanded this answer so much that it put it into the question: "Well, David, are you keeping busy?" The correct answer to all questions about work or health is "I'm very busy." If you can say it in a world-weary tone so much the better. I've come to realise that the culture I live in prizes being busy most highly. Busy defines how important we are. If we are not busy, we are not important. In this way we prize our work most highly. Our work is to be busy, our families are to be busy, our leisure is to be busy, even our parishes are to be busy.

It is socially confusing to suggest that we haven't got enough to do. To not be busy is almost to be insignificant. What matters is what we do, and what we do must keep us busy (exhausted). That is of course, until one day we are coming home from work for the last time, wondering if we matter any more.

👥 Making connections

In colluding with their captors, the Jews believed that the Samaritans represented an insult to the God of Israel and a threat to the purity of his chosen people. Amidst all this volatile tension, Jesus chose to make the Samaritan the hero of this story above the priest and Levite and thus confronted head on the prejudice of the time. There was no doubt that this story would have made some people who heard it extremely angry.

These days, the story can be interpreted in another way. Suppose the priest and the Levite who walk past the man in the ditch are not dismissive of the poor, uncaring, or fearful of an ambush. Suppose that as important and upright members of Jewish society they were just too busy to help. There are two groups who suffer when I choose to make my life busy. The first are the people I love most. The second are the poor. It is quite within me to be in so much of a hurry that I lose sight of those who need me most. Being a disciple will bring me face to face with this sort of blindness as it did the priests and Levites who heard Jesus tell the story.

As I walk into the office first thing in the morning I can be too busy. "Debbie," I say, "are the booklets ready for tomorrow's...", and then I realise what I'm doing. "Sorry," I say. "Good morning."

Conversation starters

- How often are we distracted from what is going on around us?
- Are we individually and collectively too busy?

Chapter 24

Made for each other

For just as the body is one and has many members, and all the members of the body, though many, are one body, so it is with Christ. For in the one Spirit we were all baptised into one body – Jews or Greeks, slaves or free – and we were all made to drink of one Spirit. Indeed, the body does not consist of one member but of many. If the foot would say, "Because I am not a hand, I do not belong to the body," that would not make it any less a part of the body. And if the ear would say, "Because I am not an eye, I do not belong to the body," that would not make it any less a part of the body. If the whole body were an eye, where would the hearing be? If the whole body were hearing, where would the sense of smell be? But as it is, God arranged the members in the body, each one of them, as he chose. If all were a single member, where would the body be?

1 Corinthians 12:12-19

A large group of parents had gathered that evening. The priest was delighted. "We don't usually get this many," he said. The evening seemed to go well. Afterwards, as I was packing things into the boot of my car, one of the parents came up to me in the car park. The most honest conversations tend to take place in the car park.

"I don't get it," he said. "All the Church rules seems pointless to me."

Realising that he had not spoken in the meeting, I suspected he had more to say.

"Okay," I said closing the boot and turning towards him, "what don't you get?"

"Well," he started, "I get Jesus and I'm happy with that, but I can see no reason for all the religion, the rules and regulations."

In the conversation which followed it was clear that this man had a strong personal faith, one he wanted to offer to his children. His question was whether his faith had anything to with anyone else. His quandary came from an issue which surfaces regularly. If I have God in my life, why do I need church?

It is never a bad thing to be a novice. It is good for the soul to be a beginner at something. On a previous birthday somewhere in our mid forties, Alison and I decided that our gift to each other would be the opportunity to learn a new skill. The challenge of course is that the ability to acquire new skills quickly diminishes as we get older. Like losing weight, it just gets harder to do.

Alison's present to me was a challenging two-day powerboat course leading to a certificate. This would mean an inevitable test at the end. Having grown up in the heart of England and as far from the sea as it is possible to get, I didn't have a nautical bone in my body. While I have always been attracted to the sea, I could hardly say that I knew the ways of the ocean.

The course was fascinating. The safety and navigation lectures reacquainted me with a geeky former love I had for maps and charts. Then we spent some time manoeuvring our powerful speedboat around the harbour. When you take your foot off the accelerator of a car it comes to a halt. A boat is different. Allowances have to be made as to how a boat will continue to move. Steadily we steer our boat between pontoons carefully negotiating the obstacles. It was hard at first. Some steering works against your basic instincts. Occasionally we'd overcompensate and reverse at speed, followed by a sharp intake of breath as we narrowly avoided someone's crazily expensive yacht.

At the end of our first day's training we were fantasising about selling everything we had to buy a boat. Sitting in the pub that evening you'd have been forgiven for thinking we were old seafarers with all our talk of navigation charts, tying different knots and depth sounders. Within a day we were old sea dogs. Beware though, enthusiasm is no indication of competence.

The next day we took the boat out on the Exe estuary. The Exe estuary is a special place. In the nineteenth century the railway companies purchased the banks on either side of the river to lay the tracks of their expanding network. This prevented the edges of the estuary from being built up and so the surrounding landscape has remained largely unspoilt. At low tide the river diminishes into a deep serpentine gully which winds its way through wide swathes of sand and silt. The mud banks are a paradise for migrating birds. At high tide the seawater rushes up the estuary and spills out across wide stretches of sand and mud.

The submarine landscape is constantly changing. The swift movement of the tides constantly redistributes the sand and silt on the estuary bed. Understanding how the water moves within the estuary and the position of the deeper water is essential knowledge for sailors and boat owners. To make matters more complicated the tidal flow in and out of the estuary is not consistent. A bank of sand out to sea holds back the water for a while, but once the tide rises above it there is a rush of the incoming water which is then funnelled through a narrow neck before it literally splays out across the estuary. Local knowledge is essential. If you get your timing wrong, your boat can find itself beached on a sandbank for six hours. Even the seabirds seem to find a stranded boat amusing.

Aware of the constantly changing tides, our instructor turned off the engine on our boat. As we sat quietly in the middle of the estuary it was clear that he wanted to teach us something important.

"Right," he began, "I'd like you to assess the situation we are in. The direction of the tide will affect how we manoeuvre through all these moored boats."

Turning to me he continued, "David, how do you know if the tide is coming in or going out?"

The question was really very simple. So simple that I rediscovered how embarrassing it is to have your ignorance exposed. I remember this feeling from my schooldays, trying desperately to avoid eye contact with the teacher.

Seeing that I was hesitating he tried to prompt some intelligent guess work: "Look around you, what evidence are we looking for?"

The idea that there was something obvious around us only served to heighten our ability to come out with nonsense.

"Is it the beach?" I said, pointing to a beach as if the instructor didn't know what one was. "Sometimes it is bigger and sometimes...". My answer petered out as I realised myself how ridiculous I sounded. "Perhaps not," I mumbled.

"The movement of the waves," said a fellow trainee enthusiastically, not taking into account how the wind can stir up and disturb the water.

The instructor resisted the temptation to humiliate us further. "Okay," he said, "the tide will change shortly; let's have a short break and we'll watch what happens."

He then proceeded to open up a flask of hot coffee as if the lesson was temporarily over.

Having dropped the anchor our boat was stationary. The only sound to interrupt our peace was the gentle lapping of the water against the side of the boat. When the wind isn't strong there is a strange muddled calm which descends on the water at high tide. For a short while the water isn't going anywhere. There is a reprieve in the frantic movement of the estuary as if nature herself takes a rest. Then the obvious happened. So obvious that one of my fellow trainees said, "Of course!" Our boat turned around. Not just ours, but hundreds of boats, slowly, regimentally, regardless of size or shape, turned upstream, bows pointing against the river's flow. Thousands of tons of water was heading out of the estuary again. An entire flotilla of boats telling us the same thing. A little basic physics. How do you know which way the tide is moving? Take a look at the moored boats. They're pointing at the answer. We passed the course. Just.

Making connections

There is a constant tension between what makes us unique and what unites us. Our lives are frequently a reflection of that tension. I recall several surveys of what parents most wanted for their children in which independence featured near the top of the list. On the other hand we want our children to have friends and to be popular. We know we need each other and yet at the same time we don't like to be dependent on each other.

On a visit to a school one day the principal lamented the gradual dislocation of her staff, one from another: "They've all bought kettles," she said, "and they don't come out of their classrooms." She reminisced about the "old days" when her staff room was a place of bonding and ideas. She banned the use of individual kettles to try and stem the tide!

Similarly, in religious circles there is a strong temptation to replace gathering together with privatised spirituality. The man in the car park wanted a private experience of God, one he would not have to share. As soon as tensions arise it is tempting to walk away, to do our own thing. This is not new. The New Testament includes several letters written to communities imploring them to hold on to what unites them.

What unites us best is a common direction. Communities which have a strong sense of direction tend to overcome the frequent irritations which cause us to want to go our own way. Any parish community, organisation or staff will have a much greater chance of progress if its purpose motivates it. The analogy of the body referred to by St Paul in his writing to the Corinthians is not just a call to unity, it is also a call to purpose. The analogy works because the body can't achieve its purpose in bits and pieces. A body made up of many parts can achieve something more beautiful.

Like the moored boats we are happiest aligned to each other, synchronised, and pointing in the same direction. We remain unique like the boats of different shapes and sizes, yet we are stronger in the knowledge of a shared hope for the future, reassured by the conviction of one another. Heading off in our direction isn't of itself a bad thing and it may well be gratifying for a while, but ultimately it's a lonely route. Next time you are in a church wondering why you are there, think of a flotilla of boats rather than paddling your own canoe. We are made for each other.

Conversation starters

- What is easier, doing our own thing or working in groups?
- What might be the benefit of being part of a church or organisation?

Chapter 25

Where were you?

But when Herod's birthday came, the daughter of Herodias danced before the company, and she pleased Herod so much that he promised on oath to grant her whatever she might ask. Prompted by her mother, she said, "Give me the head of John the Baptist here on a platter." The king was grieved, yet out of regard for his oaths and for the guests, he commanded it to be given; he sent and had John beheaded in the prison. The head was brought on a platter and given to the girl, who brought it to her mother. His disciples came and took the body and buried it; then they went and told Jesus. Now when Jesus heard this, he withdrew from there in a boat to a deserted place by himself. But when the crowds heard it, they followed him on foot from the towns. When he went ashore, he saw a great crowd; and he had compassion for them and cured their sick.

Matthew 14:6-14

Sometimes the news reaches us before we switch on the television in the evening. These moments occasionally turn out to be significant historical events but it is rare to realise it at the time. A few days in my life have been like that. It's easy to remember the section of road I was driving along in Plymouth one September afternoon when I heard the commentator on the radio declare, "Something is happening in New York which will change all our lives forever." The shock turned into bewilderment when the second plane flew into the twin towers. We lost some of our innocence as it dawned on us that we were no longer witnessing a tragic accident that day. One sunny Sunday morning I can still hear the vicar in a quaint Oxfordshire village church announcing the death of Diana, Princess of Wales, shortly before a baptism service was about to begin. Moments like these are indelibly etched into our memories.

For many people Dunblane was another such moment. On 13 March 1996, Thomas Hamilton walked into a Dunblane primary school and murdered sixteen children and their teacher. The event caused a long and painful re-evaluation of ourselves, our culture and about who we have become. Hamilton was an extreme but sadly not unique case of a lonely misfit choosing notoriety over a life of perceived insignificance. Until then we thought this sort of thing only happened in America.

That same week I was working in a primary school in Scunthorpe, a steel town in the east of England. The governors and staff in the school were trying to evaluate whether as a Catholic school it was noticeably and genuinely different to other schools in the area. They had asked me to help them evaluate themselves. Each morning that week I was mingling with parents at the school gate to ask questions about the school, its ethos, and the impact it was having on the families who chose to be part of it. There was a desire in the school to offer something distinctive, but in what ways?

Like so many other schools, the daily arrival of children was a frantic ritual. Cars vying for parking spaces, reversing in and out, congesting narrow streets near the school gate. Parents desperate to get on, their minds distracted by what lay ahead that day. Trying to interrupt people's routines at this time in the morning to ask a few questions doesn't make you popular. Instead I chose to conduct my survey after school, when parents might be in slightly less of a hurry.

The afternoon ritual had a certain rhythm to it. There would be those who got there early to get a good parking space, sitting in their cars reading texts. There would be others clustering in small friendship groups, an occasional burst of laughter coming from them. There would be smaller breakaway groups intent on catching up with some serious gossip. Grandparents arriving too, helping out with the children, but not very aware of where they should stand. Despite the casual appearance of it all these people stood in pretty much the same places each day, as if there was some subtle orthodoxy behind it.

The apparent calm was shattered abruptly. Children ran out of various doors and there was immediate mayhem. Shouts of "Pick up your bag it is dragging on the wet ground", "Where is your coat?" "Leave Josh alone and come over here", "Hurry up, we've got to pick up your sister and then get to the dentist." It was bedlam, as push chairs were folded and flung in to the backs of cars, babies cried, scuffles separated, and final shouts of "See you tomorrow." It was not easy to get near these people for bags, buggies and busyness. Within ten minutes it was over. The car park empty, litter swirling, and silence.

On 13 March people had heard the news of the terrible events in Dunblane as they went about their daily business. Later that evening they would put on their televisions only to confirm what they had already heard. As cars arrived for the school pickup I was there ready to survey a few of the parents. The scene began as normal. The race for car spaces was the same as always, but as the children emerged from their classrooms something different was happening.

Unlike my other visits to the school on this afternoon there was a different mood in the air. As I stood with my clipboard and approachable manner at the ready, I was quickly conscious of feeling redundant but for a different reason. The woman nearest to me saw her little boy and crouched down to his height. "Come here," she said to him, beckoning him towards her. As he approached her innocently, she wrapped her arms around him as if to hold him there and then, never to let go. To this day I am sure that there is no safer stronger more secure place in the universe than to be a child enveloped in the arms of a loving mother. It was perhaps inappropriate to listen, but she made no effort to whisper. In this intimate moment she said to him, "Something happened today which frightened me, and you must always know that I love you very much."

To my astonishment what was happening in front of me was happening behind me and across from me; in fact, throughout the playground I saw the same thing again and again. Parents had been made painfully aware of the deeper privileges of their lives, and were making public their affection for their children as if no one else was watching. That afternoon love's embrace made a mockery of the daily routine. Coat sleeves were dragging in puddles and it didn't seem to matter. All this was happening in Scunthorpe, a windswept hardy steel town where you might be forgiven for thinking that public displays of affection like this would be unlikely.

None of this meant much to the children. Being engulfed by a maternal embrace can be excruciatingly embarrassing. Most of the older children being hugged were anxiously looking round, straining their necks and hoping their friends weren't watching. "Mum," I heard some of them protest. Many of the children didn't recognise the importance of the message or where it had come from, but that wasn't the point. It needed to be said then, and it needs to be said now.

Making connections

In this remarkable passage, Jesus hears bad news. John the Baptist has been murdered. Jesus admires John, the one upon whom he heaps great praise, "among those born of women no one is greater than John". Herod meanwhile possesses a dangerous combination of immense power and foolishness. His weakness and authority contrive to bring about a brutal end for John. Whenever violence is exercised, the loved ones of victims are left bewildered by the senselessness of it.

Jesus' reaction to a pointless act of violence is important. Firstly, he withdraws. Jesus loved John. Bad news takes time to hear and accept. He must hear the news again and in solitude. Some grieving has to be done alone. The crowds though come looking for Jesus. When he returns they make demands on him. If there was something John the Baptist understood it was the crowd, searching for truth, following him into the wilderness. Like John, Jesus recognised the hunger of people longing for a visionary, someone to show them the way. In the shadow of grief for John, we hear of Jesus' compassion for a crowd who look lost and leaderless. Jesus moves through grief to compassion.

Suffering and loss can lead us not just into the pain itself, but beyond it into greater love. When we witness the suffering of others it can lead us to a deeper conviction that we will love harder, endure harder, campaign harder. There is something about an encounter with the suffering of others that can lead people to a stronger resolve for goodness.

It would have been little comfort to the people of Dunblane, and I would never have offered it as such, but all over Scotland, England, indeed all over the world, people recognised that to be a parent is a privilege rather than a right, and out of compassion resolved to express greater love for their children. In the wake of such a pointless act of violence people everywhere determined that it is in all our hands to prevent such tragedies. The healing begins by ensuring that the people we love know it. Scenes like the one I witnessed in Scunthorpe were happening everywhere, because in tragedy we recognise our shared humanity. Compassion is close behind the grieving, ready to begin the slow process of healing.

Conversation starters

- When has the suffering of others made an impact upon us?
- How can the tragedy and suffering we see around us help us to be more human?

Chapter 26

The reluctant disciple 2

Once while Jesus was standing beside the lake of Gennesaret, and the crowd was pressing in on him to hear the word of God, he saw two boats there at the shore of the lake; the fishermen had gone out of them and were washing their nets. He got into one of the boats, the one belonging to Simon, and asked him to put out a little way from the shore. Then he sat down and taught the crowds from the boat. When he had finished speaking, he said to Simon, "Put out into the deep water and let down your nets for a catch." Simon answered, "Master, we have worked all night long but have caught nothing. Yet if you say so, I will let down the nets." When they had done this, they caught so many fish that their nets were beginning to break. So they signalled their partners in the other boat to come and help them. And they came and filled both boats, so that they began to sink. But when Simon Peter saw it, he fell down at Jesus' knees, saying, "Go away from me, Lord, for I am a sinful man!" For he and all who were with him were amazed at the catch of fish that they had taken; and so also were James and John, sons of Zebedee, who were partners with Simon. Then Jesus said to Simon, "Do not be afraid; from now on you will be catching people." When they had brought their boats to shore, they left everything and followed him.

Luke 5:1-11

The sleet on Bodmin Moor comes at you horizontally. Late at night on the A38, there have been times when I could barely see through the windscreen. It is wonderful to work in the West Country but during the short days of midwinter, late-night journeys on slow narrow roads can be tedious. Imagine then my excitement at being invited to lead a couple of workshops under the cloudless blue skies of Los Angeles. The prospect of a blast of vitamin D in February was enticing. The invitation was too good an opportunity to miss as there was the sniff of an adventure in the air. For the first time I would visit California, a state that had entertained the world for a hundred years and redefined the way we tell stories. LA is the imagination capital of the world. I felt sure that I'd learn more than I would teach, that I would receive more than I would give. As it turned out, I was right. Much more so than I could have ever imagined.

With eager anticipation I put together a carefully crafted PowerPoint presentation. To accompany it I printed fifty handouts for each workshop, reread a few of the sources I was quoting, practised my delivery, tested my timing, and set off for Heathrow Airport. It was flattering to be invited to a conference on the other side of the world and it would give me a chance to learn from other speakers, many of whom had written the books on my shelves.

The Religious Education Congress in Anaheim, Orange County, is not like any other event I have attended. Arriving early for my workshop I was surprised to find myself in a hotel ballroom with a team of sound technicians, grand chandeliers, water dispensers and seating for a thousand people. This was an enormous space for a little workshop, row upon row of seats all linked to each other and a podium mounted on a stage at the front. As several people arrived I invited them to come forward. "Please come and join me at the front," I said. "We'll use the front couple of rows." Within ten minutes a thousand people were sitting in front of me and at least another twenty-nine thousand people were heading for other workshops. Some people were standing at the back. It occurred to me that we needed a multiplication miracle if the worksheets were going to be of any use, so they stayed in the box by my feet. "Well," I began, "where I come from we'd call this a city not a conference."

At the twilight of each day ten thousand people would gather for Mass in an arena built for sport. The whole space was transformed by colourful drapes hung from the ceiling, an enormous temporary stage with a spectacular backdrop, a full orchestra and choir, gantries of lighting, two massive video screens, stacks of audio speakers and ten thousand people. The atmosphere in the arena was one of anticipation. Standing in one of the aisles watching people take their seats I became very aware that this was not my home. It all felt unfamiliar. The regular attenders raced for the front seats placing their bags and coats on them like a towel on a sunbed. In an arena of ten thousand people it was easy to go to the upper levels and slip quietly into a hiding place on the back row. I was reluctant to sit anywhere near the front. Upstairs I would not be drawn into anything I didn't understand. Like Zacchaeus up the tree, I could watch from a distance. There would be no commitment, no coming down.

Powerful Vietnamese drummers called us to attention. After a stunning silence, the choir began to sing. The lyrics spoke of gathering together in the presence of God. Something important was about to happen. Into the arena processed a long line of servers, deacons, priests, bishops and finally the cardinal. The procession was accompanied by bold, confident music. Nothing was casual about what was happening. The choreography was flawless, rehearsed in every detail. This was Christian, but not as I knew it, not English reserved Christianity. This was assertive, unashamed, enthusiastic, colourful and confident. This was LA.

What took me completely by surprise were the dancers, some carrying large bowls of incense. They were both athletic and graceful, their movements careful and deliberate. They unfolded themselves in precise movements while their faces expressed sincerity. These people were praying through movement like David, who had danced enthusiastically before the Ark of the Lord.

It was the men, whose physique was athletic and whose actions were delicate, that intrigued me the most. It was strange for me. On the one hand I was impressed by their conviction and their obvious belief in what they were doing. On the other hand I was aware of my roots. As I watched I was mindful of Ilkeston where I lived at that time, a coalmining town in the East Midlands. This was the neighbourhood of authors like D. H. Lawrence, where small gritty industrial towns like neighbouring Eastwood spawned mining men who did not express themselves through the creative arts. Lawrence wrote of brutal men, men who lived in the shadows of their fathers and who like them would carve out a harsh existence in the coalpits. Even though the pits had long gone, I couldn't think of a single man in any of these dirty old industrial towns who would dance like that into a place of worship. Not one. Something about the dancers made me glad I had a back row seat.

On the second day of this remarkable event curiosity brought me to a seat closer to the front, a place where I could get a better look. I seated myself tight left of the stage where several rows of seats remained empty. The view of the raised staging was slightly impaired from there, which I suspected led to the unpopularity of these seats. Surreptitiously I slid into one of these rows where I could observe more closely the whole liturgy: the faces of the people presiding, the musicians and the dancers. Safely hidden, I could watch and learn. As I was the day before, I was safe here also.

The second Mass was prepared by the African-American community. It would be an experience of black American worship. Everyone involved in leading this liturgy was black. The proceedings began with two women who calmly positioned themselves on the stage and then effortlessly filled the auditorium with the most powerful voices. It could have been Etta James or Aretha Franklin singing. It was an electric moment. The conductor of the orchestra stood next to them and proceeded to animate the musicians. By now the presiding priest had processed in and behind him were those perplexing dancers, their faces visible. Here their movements appeared more defined and graceful.

Conviction is attractive. It is admirable to be able to shake off criticism or the fear of failure because you believe in what you are doing. There have been many people in my life I have admired because of the strength of their conviction. Whether this dancing is entertainment or worship has been the subject of much contention, and yet sitting before it I saw an authentic prayer expressed in the faces of these people. You don't dance in holy places unless you have conviction. Despite a growing appreciation for a style of prayer so different to my own, never in a million years would you get me doing something like that. No! Appreciating is one thing, participating is another.

What happened next took me by surprise. The movement stopped, so too the music. There was total silence and an atmosphere of solemnity. Out of the silence the conductor moved across the stage towards me, and fixing his stare directly upon me, pointed in my direction with both hands. He then opened his hands, palms upright and raised them both upwards, as if to beckon me to stand. "Me, why me?" I said to myself. Why did he want me to stand in front of ten thousand people? Did he know I was English? Was this one of those terrifying altar calls? Were they going to pray for me? Tentatively, nervously, timidly, I slowly stood up as if to receive a verdict in a courtroom. Staring directly back at him, I was now doing exactly what I'd hoped to avoid. I was participating.

The sound of perfect harmony resounded back at him from all around me. It was only then that I realised I was in the choir. Twisting my head first to the right then left, I now saw that I was surrounded by about sixty singers, each of them wearing the same red top, each of them black. There was a sign above me which read "Choir only". Why hadn't I noticed it before? Now I realised why such well-positioned seats had remained empty. The choir had been practising this moment for six months and on their night when all their labours came to fruition, in the middle of them appeared an awkward lemon from England.

The choir was abundantly joyful. Their collective sound was uplifting, a truly beautiful cacophony. They swayed from side to side, dipping their heads from right to left as they did so. Those nearest me saw my awkward predicament and gestured as if to encourage me to sway with them. Unlike the natural rhythm of this beautifully choreographed group, I cautiously went with them. It was the least I could do. Even though I was in time with them, I was a wooden Anglo Saxon. I'm sure I have never felt so white. Despite my awkwardness their skill and joyfulness was enough to help me lose myself. With a little enthusiasm now, I was starting to sway, dipping my head to the right and then to the left as if for a brief moment I was really one of them. Gradually I caught myself enjoying the moment, I was becoming African-American from downtown LA.

Having consoled myself that being beside the stage, sideways on, no one from the auditorium could see me, I now realised that above the stage was a huge video screen and the cameraman had found me. My total lack of grace and elegance was there for all to see, like Mr Bean in a ballet. This was not pretty at all. A ripple of laughter worked its way around the whole arena as people pointed out the white guy in the choir. In the space of just one day, I had managed to go from the upper tier back row to video screen. The day before I had sat at the back of an arena determined not to participate. The next day I was Captain Ridiculous on the video screen, pretending to know the words of the hymn I was singing and moving like a drunk uncle at a wedding. This was not what I set out to do. Is this what coming here was meant to give me?

👥 Making connections

My reluctance to stand up and participate is ultimately what this book is about. Reluctance comes from a variety of fears within us. Fear of not knowing enough, fear of being out of control, fear of other people, fear of being a fool – there are so many fears to overcome. One of our fears is of love itself. Confronted by love some of us fall into our own unworthiness and hide. Like Peter, we reject the idea that God loves us because we feel we should have deserved it or earn it in some way. Peter had learned to fish by his own efforts. We begin to believe that we should merit God's love in the same way. Jesus reveals his love for Peter in the abundance of fish Peter catches. Peter realises that by his own efforts he can never merit such a catch. His pride pushes Jesus away.

There is a serious me that wants God on my terms. Pride will push away the love of God and I can fill the space with all sorts of concerted effort, duty and devotions as if I should earn it before I receive it. My devotion is a response to God's generosity, not a precondition for it. Finally after all my efforts have failed I come to him empty handed, a fool, not in control of events and in that space he whispers, "Do not be afraid."

Discipleship sounds like a job. It isn't. It is a walk in the footsteps of Jesus. If we decide to follow him, he will take us on a journey from the upper tier of the back row, down into the mess and confusion of people's lives and into the face of our own limitations. Among these things he teaches us. Sometimes we will find ourselves in the unexpected spaces, perhaps being laughed at, and often in these moments he reaches beyond our pride. The alternative is serious, po-faced, respectable and ultimately reluctant discipleship. Sitting at the back of the arena, upstairs, I served no one but myself.

As a young man I once asked my dad what was the most important lesson life had taught him and he told me simply,

"Don't take yourself too seriously." He was right. The dance in Anaheim was an expression of joy. Joy is not something to take seriously. Like the catch of fish, we should accept it when we see it, dare to join it occasionally, and recognise it isn't about us anyway.

Conversation starters

- What reluctance puts us off stepping forward and choosing the front seats?
- What helps us to overcome our fear of failure or embarrassment?

Chapter 27

Hidden in the everything

Indeed, there have to be factions among you, for only so will it become clear who among you are genuine. When you come together, it is not really to eat the Lord's supper. For when the time comes to eat, each of you goes ahead with your own supper, and one goes hungry and another becomes drunk. What! Do you not have homes to eat and drink in? Or do you show contempt for the church of God and humiliate those who have nothing? What should I say to you? Should I commend you? In this matter I do not commend you! For I received from the Lord what I also handed on to you, that the Lord Jesus on the night when he was betrayed took a loaf of bread, and when he had given thanks, he broke it and said, "This is my body that is for you. Do this in remembrance of me." In the same way he took the cup also, after supper, saying, "This cup is the new covenant in my blood. Do this, as often as you drink it, in remembrance of me." For as often as you eat this bread and drink the cup, you proclaim the Lord's death until he comes. So then, my brothers and sisters, when you come together to eat, wait for one another. If you are hungry, eat at home, so that when you come together, it will not be for your condemnation. About the other things I will give instructions when I come.

1 Corinthians 11:19-26. 33-34

I t was an intriguing title in the Letters page of our local paper which caught my eye. It read simply, "You can keep the car." The statement didn't make much sense. To whom was it addressed? The intrigue got the better of me. Reading the brief letter below, it continued, "You can keep the Silver BMW 3 Series you stole last Thursday from outside my home on Nottingham Road." The letter then took on a completely different tone. "In the glove compartment," it continued, "was a letter from my father, it was the last thing he ever gave to me." The writer continued with a brief description of her father and what he meant to her and then the letter finished on a more assertive tone, "You can keep the car, give me back the letter, it is worthless to you!" On a page of several trite and trivial letters, the writer had revealed something profound. It was a true demonstration about the greater value of things, yet we remain so easily fooled by their monetary worth. Good taste is confused with how much something costs rather than what it means to us.

A more dramatic and well-known demonstration of this took place on a beach close to my home. On 18 January 2007 a container ship the MSC Napoli was heading for Portugal when severe storms cracked the hull and flooded her engine room. The crew of thirty-one had to abandon the ship leaving her to the mercy of the sea. The next day the ship was towed along the English Channel towards a safe harbour. Continuing her journey she began to list drastically to one side. A controversial decision was made to beach the ship in Lyme Bay, where the leakage of oil could be restricted and a salvage operation begin. She sat a mile off the coast, undignified and precarious on a shallow submerged ledge, her 62,000 tonnes tilting drastically to starboard. As winds picked up again, the huge containers she carried began to slide one by one off her deck and into the coastal waters. These containers were tossed about in the tide and washed up at nearby Branscombe in Devon. On 20 January, broken containers revealed all manner of items including nappies, dog food, cosmetics, car parts, oak wine barrels, motorbikes and Bibles, lots of them in Polish. All manner of bags, boxes and objects found their way onto the pebble beach.

What happened next caught the attention of the press worldwide. People travelled from as far as three hundred miles away, in what one newspaper described as, "The greatest free-for-all since the glory days of Devon's eighteenth-century wreckers." In the eighteenth century, flotsam (the term given to floating wreckage) was believed to be the property of the finder. In the coastal counties of Devon and Cornwall, unscrupulous scavengers would use lamplight to misguide sailing ships onto hidden rocks so that their cargoes could become fair game. These became known as wreckers. Other newspapers described the so-called wreckers as "fortune hunters" in the "great Devon take away."

As news spread of the free-for-all, more and more people headed south to descend upon that tiny stretch of beach and the rich pickings to be found there. For three days the press reported the spillage as a windfall, a piece of good fortune for those lucky enough to come across it, and the police made few attempts to stop the scavenging. People happily spoke to reporters and journalists as they rummaged through containers and boxes to see what bounty they could acquire.

On 23 January everything changed. Anita and Jan Bokdal's possessions were being transported from their native Sweden to South Africa on the Napoli. In the reports of the scavenging they saw pictures of their own family heirlooms, family photographs, clothes and a precious tea set being opened up, examined, discarded or stolen. One newspaper reported their distress and the mood began to change. The next day the police branded the scavenging as "despicable" and promptly closed the beach, erected high fences around the site and announced that they would use recent legislation to make people return the goods or face prosecution. The party was over. Once it became clear that the goods included personal belongings and not merely goods for sale, the newspapers began talking about "organised gangs in vans", "theft" and "greed" rather than a "free-for-all" by "fortune hunters". Could it be that the sight of a damaged tea set in a newspaper article is powerful enough to change the way people see things?

🧑 Making connections

Emily's great-grandmother sent her a card. There were ninety lived years between their ages. It was a small card, with a picture of a cat on the front. It had a small note inside with some kind words. What struck me was her final sentence. She wrote simply, "I saw this picture of a cat and thought you might like it." We read the card to Emily and she inspected the picture carefully. In a second the card was on the table, and then with the draft of an open door it was on the kitchen floor. I picked it up quickly and stood it on the mantelpiece. I imagined that when Emily's great-grandmother was a little girl she would have kept a card like that in a small Victorian toffee tin under her bed. It would have been a piece of her personal treasure in a tiny treasure chest. By contrast Emily, even at the age of six, was able to go online, choose a breed of cat and press print. Yet no picture of a cat emerging out of our printer would ever have been worth trading for that card.

Catholics look at the world through a sacramental lens. St Augustine in the fifth century described a sacrament as "An outward and visible sign of an inward and invisible grace." The Church gave the title of sacrament to particular moments when what appears to be something quite ordinary possesses a greater and transformative presence. For Augustine, the sacraments not only carried something hidden, they had a capacity to change, heal and enable people.

We have this sense naturally, it is in our bones. It is why we irrationally hold onto things and store them in our lofts. The thing itself may be quite worthless, but to us it is valuable because it makes present something more profound than what we see. People who don't understand it will not see it. They will just see a furless teddy bear or an antique locket with a picture of an old lady in it. It looks to them like a worthless envelope in the glove compartment of a high-performance car. It is something to throw away or sell in a car boot sale.

When St Paul chastises the Corinthians he is instructing them not to trample upon that deeper sense of sacrament. He implores them not to turn the Lord's Supper into something casual. In the passage, the community in Corinth is challenged to recognise something more profound than the fending off of hunger pangs. Paul reminds them that at the Last Supper Jesus gave a special significance to the breaking of bread and the drinking of wine. To those who see it, the meal carries a presence which can transform and change people; to those who don't, it's just a meal.

A sacramental lens can help us to begin to recognise the sacredness in everything. It draws us more deeply into the mysteries of life until, without our earning it, working for it, deserving it or fully comprehending it, our entire life becomes a sacrament, an outward sign of an inward presence. We begin to recognise the hallmarks of God's intervention in our lives, our struggles and our accomplishments.

Jesus gave us the sign of bread and wine so that he would be present to us. St Paul calls upon us to approach that gift with care, because once you recognise it you know that there is more to what you receive than you can understand or imagine. God becomes present to us in the ordinary stuff of life. Once you see it, you begin to see it everywhere, in the glove compartment of a stolen car or in a broken tea set on a beach. You can keep the car, give her back the letter!

Conversation starters

- What makes something valuable or worth keeping?
- What does it mean to describe something as sacred?

Chapter 28

Organ soup

He entered Jericho and was passing through it. A man was there named Zacchaeus; he was a chief tax collector and was rich. He was trying to see who Jesus was, but on account of the crowd he could not, because he was short in stature. So he ran ahead and climbed a sycamore tree to see him, because he was going to pass that way. When Jesus came to the place, he looked up and said to him, "Zacchaeus, hurry and come down; for I must stay at your house today." So he hurried down and was happy to welcome him. All who saw it began to grumble and said, "He has gone to be the guest of one who is a sinner." Zacchaeus stood there and said to the Lord, "Look, half of my possessions, Lord, I will give to the poor; and if I have defrauded anyone of anything, I will pay back four times as much." Then Jesus said to him, "Today salvation has come to this house, because he too is a son of Abraham. For the Son of Man came to seek out and to save the lost."

Luke 19:1-10

In the dry rolling hills above the city of Jos in northern Nigeria lies the small village of Dis. It is so tiny a settlement that it barely features on the maps. The road that leads there leads nowhere else. The village consists of several brightly painted brick-built houses, some of them two storeys high with corrugated tin roofs. There is a church, a classroom, several clusters of houses, an open square for gatherings, chickens, a few goats and not much else. This simple tiny plateau village was to be my home for a few days.

What remains so memorable about my visit there was my arrival. Arriving by minibus from Jos, I was surrounded by an entire village who had come to meet their visitor. The priest, Fr Joseph, who was to be my host, greeted me like an old friend. Then there were the hordes of children, lots of them staring at my pale skin as though I was from another planet. They reached out nervously to me, and as I reached out in reply they withdrew as if touching my hand might be dangerous. It took a few minutes before they were climbing all over me. The majority of inhabitants here were peasant farmers with enough to feed themselves and their families, with a little to spare. This was not a desperate place. The rainfall was sustaining life in the fields and plenty of it was lush, but the overall impression was of a village community that had little more than what it needed to survive.

My room was sparse by Western standards. There was a bed, a desk, a lamp and an intermittent power supply. There was also an en suite bathroom of sorts – a room adjoining my own which had a hole in one corner and a very large plastic bucket filled with water. As my host explained, I could use the water to wash, shower and to wash away my excrement. It would be refilled for me once a day. What a luxury a tap is.

That evening I gave a presentation to the parish council. Fr Joseph was there, along with thirty men of the village sitting in tight rows on benches. They sat to attention in what felt like a mood of total deference. Standing before them I felt the long shadow of colonial history hanging over our meeting. The British had ruled here until 1960, and although many of these men would not remember the arrival of independence, their parents would have lived in a colony. Entwined with all that of course was the presence of the Catholic and Protestant missions which brought Christianity to the region. Whether I liked it or not, we were sitting in the shadow of a bigger story than ours. Our meeting could not escape its black and white history.

The group seemed reserved, unwilling to raise or answer questions. The subservience brought with it obedience but much less in the way of genuine engagement. At the conclusion of the session, Fr Joseph said, "David would like to hear any questions." There were none. The men looked to the floor. A polite silence hung over us until he pointed to one of the men and said, "Ask Mr Wells a question." To my surprise the man stood up, and proceeded almost immediately to ask me something. It was as if he had it ready, but could barely bring himself to ask it with any confidence. "Mr Wells, sir," he began, "in England, how much do people give from their earnings to help others?" It was a question which laid bare the strangeness of this situation. After giving a feeble response I was then duly thanked for my work and the men kindly applauded.

After years of curiosity and cynicism, of applauding and heckling, of people appreciating or objecting to what I teach, the deference I experienced in that most humble of circumstances was a clash of cultures that left me uncomfortable. I couldn't accept it because I didn't deserve it. I walked away ashamed of myself for presuming to teach them things they already knew. That night I lay in bed wondering what on earth I was doing there. I didn't sleep at all.

The next day was Sunday. Despite the dust and dirt that blew in the breeze, the men and women gathered for Mass in their smartest outfits. The women wore turquoise, yellow or blue dresses they wrapped around themselves, called Abaya. They looked beautiful every one of them, in vibrant colours on their black skin. From miles and miles around they came. For hours and hours they walked, until the entire square was teeming with people. Once gathered, Mass began and everyone started to dance. The children danced, the choir danced, the priest danced, even the elderly danced and they did so not apart but together. This was not dancing to impress. It was prompted by unbridled joy and it was impossible not to dance with them. The service lasted for three hours. At its conclusion they carried the young curate who had presided at Mass out of the square on their shoulders because they were proud of him. Overwhelmed by the celebration, my feelings of inadequacy were compounded. Coming here as a teacher was sheer presumption. I was their pupil.

As my last night in this village approached there was to be a party for me in thanksgiving for my visit. The last thing I needed was their gratitude; I'd been rewarded enough. If I had learned anything though, it was to accept with humility whatever they offered me. As I sat down at the table they had prepared they gave me a hand-written menu. As a guest of honour I could choose my meal. Appreciating their efforts I chose something I recognised, the soup. There were a few things I had eaten in Nigeria which had had unforeseen consequences. On my last night I went for the safe familiar option. What could be safer than soup?

When the soup came out it had the look of a collection of animal organs in tepid water. The organs had tubes. Most of them floating. This meal had been offered with love, and meat of any kind here is to be prized. There was no sending it back. Looking at it though, my Western pallet was drying up, my stomach knotting. Everything except my conscience was telling me to run for it. My stomach began to reach in anticipation; I could hear it protesting: "You're not sending that down here." In an attempt to harpoon one of the organs with a fork, it popped and spat back at me, before deflating slowly. Then, lifting the fork to my mouth I knew that all I could do was recall the prospect of eating sprouts as a child and the method I adopted then. I would chew aggressively and swallow the sprout as quickly as I could. That is what I did, chewed aggressively and swallowed quickly. Although the taste was quite insipid, it was the texture which made it hard to swallow. I doubt I will ever again be as grateful for a bottle of Nigerian lager as I was that night.

As the minibus approached to pick me up, my new friends gathered around me to say goodbye. As I threw my rucksack into the back of the van and prepared to climb in, Fr Joseph took my shoulder in his hand and said, "David, you are a true missionary." Turning to look at him I apologised, "Father," I said, "it was a poor talk to your council, your men deserved better, it was inappropriate and badly delivered." He laughed. "Forget the talk," he said, "what matters is that you ate the soup."

Making connections

Meals are a regular feature of Luke's Gospel. On many occasions, the meal is the setting for a significant teaching. In Simon's house Jesus teaches about mercy (Luke 7:40-50), at the Pharisee's house he challenges self-righteousness (14:1-14), at the meal on the way to Emmaus the disciples recognise Jesus as risen from the dead (24:30-32).

Unlike these stories, the visit to Zacchaeus' home is intriguing in that we are not invited to witness the narrative at the meal. We know that Jesus choosing to stay with Zacchaeus has a transformative impact upon him. For Zacchaeus to be rich he must defraud his own people and allow the Romans to protect him. He is reviled. Jesus' visit is enough to restore Zacchaeus' integrity and he is determined to make amends for the injustices that have made him wealthy.

It is tempting to imagine that the way we learn is in the classroom. That is true of course, but the meal is the place of deeper connection. If you want to tell someone you love them, if you want to say hello or goodbye, if you need to apologise or appreciate, do it over a meal table. Meals are how we marry, how we celebrate, how we remember, how we receive Christ. Staying with Zacchaeus isn't therefore the setting of the teaching, it is the teaching.

When I visited Dis I thought we'd teach each other something in the seminar. We did, yet much more was achieved at the meal, something eternal. It turned out it was all about the soup!

Conversation starters

- What are the most memorable meals of our lives?
- Why might Jesus have chosen a meal by which to remember him?

Chapter 29

Being ridiculous

The next day the great crowd that had come to the festival heard that Jesus was coming to Jerusalem. So they took branches of palm trees and went out to meet him, shouting, "Hosanna! Blessed is the one who comes in the name of the Lord – the King of Israel!" Jesus found a young donkey and sat on it; as it is written: "Do not be afraid, daughter of Zion. Look, your king is coming, sitting on a donkey's colt!" His disciples did not understand these things at first; but when Jesus was glorified, then they remembered that these things had been written of him and had been done to him. So the crowd that had been with him when he called Lazarus out of the tomb and raised him from the dead continued to testify. It was also because they heard that he had performed this sign that the crowd went to meet him. The Pharisees then said to one another, "You see, you can do nothing. Look, the world has gone after him!"

John 12:12-19

In the early days of my teaching career I was driven by adrenalin. Each morning I woke before my alarm sounded. On the journey to work I'd have a knot in my stomach and a mixture of nervousness and excitement. I knew that to be a successful teacher wasn't going to be easy. It takes only a trapped wasp on the windowsill to spoil the best-laid lesson plan. During my first years of teaching, success meant working into the early hours of the morning five nights a week. Things can always go wrong.

On reflection, though, something else was driving me. Among the mostly inspirational teachers around me there were also a few bored teachers, some indifferent teachers and sadly a few badly burnt-out teachers. I determined not to be like any of those. It was my ambition not to be a good but to be outstanding. Like Robin Williams in *Dead Poets Society* I would change lives, inspire young people beyond their own limited and local horizons. I and the other young teachers I'd trained with shared a strong sense of vocation, a driving professional zeal. We were keen not only to be successful, but to be noticed. Success in the classroom would ultimately be our significance. We would be remembered for our pioneering endeavours in the field of pedagogy. One day the young people would stand on their desks and declare us their captain.

As light relief from all that youthful idealism and zealousness came the weekends. Friday nights were especially good. After playing football we'd head into town for a few drinks and a pizza. One Friday evening we discovered the Lincolnshire Poacher, a popular pub on the Mansfield Road in Nottingham. It was one of those pubs that attracted a variety of clientele, the well dressed, who were heading for the nearby theatre, lots of students, tradesmen calling in on their way home. It was a great pub to watch the world unwind. As a place to relax it wasn't trendy or chic. It hadn't invested in its decor. There were no low-slung designer sofas in burgundy, no table lamps or expensive wine lists. This pub focused more on its beer, with a wide assortment of local ales each with a strange name. After three pints of the local mead everyone's jokes were hilarious. After five pints we were talking absolute nonsense to people who weren't listening. It was a way of letting go.

Several years into the job, I find myself enjoying another late Friday night in the Poacher. Happily engrossed in a conversation I feel a tap on the shoulder. "Sir?" asks a deep voice behind me. Unless you have been knighted by the monarch, this title almost invariably means that the speaker is an ex-pupil. It doesn't matter how old they are, they struggle to get beyond "Sir" or "Mr Wells". These days I meet ex-pupils in their forties and they still hesitate to call me by my Christian name. My heart sinks. The tap on the shoulder is work interrupting. This is school life intruding on my private life with friends, girlfriend, and beer. The tap on my shoulder is two distinct and separate worlds colliding.

In a crowded space, tightly clutching my pint close to my chest, I turn 180 degrees on my heels. "I thought it was you, sir," says the enthusiastic voice, shouting into my ear over the self-assembled band of guitarists in the corner. For a short while his name escapes me. His face, his body, his whole demeanour has filled out. He has the look of someone in his early twenties. I listen intently for a clue to his name and then from nowhere it comes to me. The young lad I remember him as has turned into a big man with more confidence. My next reaction is to hope that we got on when he was at school! If he didn't like me as a teacher this might be his moment to tell me why I was awful, boring or unfair. But I soon realise that it's okay, he's not going to tear into me. In fact he seems truly delighted to see me. Within a few minutes he's bought me a drink and is reminiscing about his time at school, about the other teachers and says he wishes he'd worked a bit harder. His appreciation is so obvious that I quickly warm to the conversation and introduce him to my friends.

"Do you know what I most remember about you, Mr Wells?" he asks. Given his general enthusiasm, and the fact that I'm now drinking a beer he's bought me, I'm confident that I must have inspired him in some way. Perhaps all the long hours of lesson preparation, assessments, meeting targets and patient pastoral care was about to pay off. Perhaps he would mention the lively ethics debates I encouraged, or my hilarious stories, or the school trips I led, or the quizzes I organised to help them remember facts. Perhaps I'd altered the course of his life by my inspiring example. Perhaps I encouraged him to stay on the right track and rise above the demands of his peer group. Perhaps he would remind me why I am a teacher and affirm my life choice. This was to be my moment of glory. "Tell me," I said, "what is it that you remember most?"

"Do you remember when you took us on the school trip to Alton Towers with all those rollercoasters and we were late getting back to the bus at the end of the day?"

I'd forgotten the incident but his words brought back a vague memory of keeping everyone waiting while someone went to look for these boys. Unlike him, I remembered more vividly the irate parents waiting back at the school gate much later that night, and having to apologise to them all.

He carried on, "Do you remember when we got on the bus, how you were standing at the front giving us all a big lecture about consideration of others?"

"Yes," I said slowly, apprehensive about the direction this was going in.

"Well," he added with a dramatic pause, "you told everyone off and do you know something, your flies were undone!"

At this point all six foot two inches of the man fell to pieces in a fit of laughter while I stood aghast, holding his pint and mine. He kept slapping his leg as if it was the funniest thing he ever saw. He was beside himself with laughter because I had told him off with my flies undone.

"That's it?" I thought. "All that hard work and all you can remember are my flies?"

After a little more reminiscing I thanked him for the drink, he shook my hand very hard and told me that he would never forget that day on the bus – as though I would be grateful. With that he disappeared into the crowd and I heard him saying to his friend, "That bloke over there used to teach me."

👥 Making connections

It's no longer good enough to be successful. These days it's just as important to be seen to be successful. To be recognised. To be famous. Seeking appreciation is a dangerous game. Admiration of others blows where it will. It is there one minute and gone the next. It is the torment of the famous.

When the rich man asks Jesus, "Good Teacher, what must I do to inherit eternal life?" Jesus' response is, "Why do you call me good? No one is good but God alone" (Luke 18:18-19). Jesus is refuting the man's flattery. He is resisting his admiration. It is a lesson Jesus will teach more graphically when he enters Jerusalem. In fulfilling the prophecy in Zechariah 9:9 Jesus rides into Jerusalem not on a stallion as Pontius Pilate had done, but on a donkey. The crowds miss the irony. They continue to offer their adulation. If he were to debase himself by pleasing the crowd he would become subject to them. In Matthew 4:5-7, Jesus resists the temptation to be impressive by refusing to jump off the parapet in front of the crowds. He would not fall prey to it now. He did not go to Jerusalem to be admired.

Wanting to be a good teacher was noble; wanting to be an impressive teacher was vanity. The young man in the pub was teaching me something important. Very few people I have taught have thanked me for the information I gave them. Despite every manner of assessment being focused on performance indicators, the truth is that people mainly remember what they liked or disliked about us. For all the effort we put into pushing up students' results, and as important as all that is, what really influences people is something else. To some extent this is true of all relationships. We tend to remember how it was rather than what it was. We don't remember the waitress giving us the food, but we do remember whether she was cheerful or sullen.

While God holds each one of us as precious, it is important not to lose sight of the fact that we are all a bit ridiculous. Whenever I forget that and start to take myself too seriously I think of my friend in the Poacher. While I was busy trying to prove myself all he could see was a clown with his flies undone.

Conversation starters

- Is there something crazy about wanting to be appreciated or famous?
- Is it valuable to have a sense of our own ridiculousness?

Chapter 30

Left on the shelf

If you love me, you will keep my commandments. And I will ask the Father, and he will give you another Advocate, to be with you forever. This is the Spirit of truth, whom the world cannot receive, because it neither sees him nor knows him. You know him, because he abides with you, and he will be in you. I will not leave you orphaned; I am coming to you. In a little while the world will no longer see me, but you will see me; because I live, you also will live. On that day you will know that I am in my Father, and you in me, and I in you. They who have my commandments and keep them are those who love me; and those who love me will be loved by my Father, and I will love them and reveal myself to them.

John 14:15-21

For me statues have always held a certain fascination. A skilful sculpture allows us to concentrate upon a single expression frozen in time. Charles I'Anson's figure of Christ hanging in the chapel at Leeds Trinity University is a striking example. I'Anson's Christ is in agony, heaving himself away from the cross in order to breathe. So graphic is the sculpture that the first time I saw it I was tempted to look away. Few depictions of a crucifixion portray the grotesque nature of the torture the way this does. This is Christ giving of himself in a supreme act of love. There is no defeat in the sculpture, yet the face of Christ is crying out in lonely anguish. Statues are not idols, their purpose is to draw us more closely to who or what they represent.

Michelangelo's Pietà is of course a much more famous piece. In beautiful Carrara marble Jesus' mother cradles his body after the crucifixion. The ripples in Mary's garments give the sculpture a sense of motion. She grips tightly the body of her crucified son with her right hand, her left hand extended and opened in a gesture of pleading grief. We are reminded of Simeon's prophecy that a sword would one day pierce the heart of Mary. The sculpture takes us into that moment. So accurately captured is the posture of a mother in sorrow that I have seen it repeated several times in scenes of tragedy on the news.

The fascination with statues probably goes back to a childhood visit to Madame Tussauds. The inanimate models were eerily accurate as if trapping a life inside. As a teacher I later went back with a group of pupils. In a moment of mischief I found an empty alcove in the Chamber of Horrors exhibition, and climbing over the rope stood inside motionless. People peered at me searching for a plaque to establish my identity. Much to the delight of my students, when I stepped forward to rejoin my group, two women screamed as if I had come to life that very moment, there and then.

For a while St Mary's was a school I visited regularly to work with the teachers and parents. It was a charming happy little primary school tucked away behind a large housing estate. By and large everything went on smoothly there. The staff did a good job, the parents appreciated the school and it performed well in assessments. By its own admission, though, it had become a little too comfortable and resistant to change. Since there were few problems it had become tempting not to innovate. As a consequence the school had become static.

The reception area at St Mary's had the typical arrangement of furniture. A cabinet with some trophies, two sofas for waiting visitors, a couple of large pots containing carefully nurtured plants and a display of pupils' artwork. High up, above the sliding glass which separated the reception from the secretary's office, was a large shelf supporting a statue of Mary, the Mother of Jesus. It was easy not to notice the image. She too was static and largely out of view.

One morning while waiting to meet the school principal my attention was drawn to the statue. Mary was represented in the traditional style, wearing a white gown with a blue mantle. She had a gold belt around her waist and a white veil. Her arms were outstretched as if she was trying to communicate something. Her expression was slightly forlorn, a hint of sadness perhaps. The combination of that expression and her posture gave the statue an air of disapproval. She was looking down upon us. How could she do anything else, she was so high up?

As the school's feast day approached, I had been asked to lead a morning assembly on the theme of Mary, the Mother of Jesus. "Let's get the statue down," I said, "and use it for what it was meant, to help us teach." Perhaps we could use the statue to move things along a bit, I thought. With the caretaker we manhandled the sculpture off the shelf and unceremoniously down a ladder. Two things struck me. Firstly, this was a heavy statue and not at all as fragile as she appeared on the shelf. Secondly, she was bigger than she appeared mounted so high on the wall. She was also a little grubby for years of dust and cobwebs. A careful clean would brighten her.

Small children are a challenge to me. I'm comfortable with sullen monosyllabic teenagers or cynical adults, but small children require a completely different skillset. They are over-enthusiastic, unpredictable and easily distracted, characteristics which don't work well together.

My intention was to tell them a story about their patron saint, so I began by placing the statue amongst them on the hall floor. As each class came into the hall with their teacher they sat around her, having never been so close up to the statue. We said an opening prayer and then I asked them who the statue was. A sea of hands shot into the air, desperate to please me. "Mary," shouted one, unable to contain his expert knowledge. "That's right," I said. "Where did Mary live?" I asked, to see if we could put the pieces of her story together. The hands went up again. "On the shelf near the door," said a voice from close beside me. This was going to be a long morning.

After several questions about what Mary did and why the school might be named after her, I thought I would exploit the statue a little more. Knowing how observant children can be I asked them to look closely at her face. "What do you think Mary is thinking?" I knew this question could lead us anywhere. Fewer hands were raised now. One of the older children said, "She looks worried." "What do you think she is worried about?" I asked. Another pause, and then one of the smaller children said with a heavy, world-weary sigh, "Probably Jesus." The teachers laughed. "Why would she worry about Jesus?" I said. "He runs away to church without telling his mum," another child proffered – which I presumed was a reference to the famous story of losing Jesus in the Temple when he was a boy. They were now seeing this statue as if she represented someone like their own mother, someone who would worry about Jesus the way their own mums would worry about them. The woman represented here is now a mother who loved her son. Her posture and expression are no longer disapproving.

We listened to a reading, paused for a while and the music teacher led us in a hymn after which the older children started to file out of the hall. As they did so the formal atmosphere of the hall was broken, and the children began to whisper quietly to each other. More fascinating was the behaviour of the smallest children, who were yet to be called to leave. They slowly edged themselves forward until they got as close to the statue as they dared. Almost lost to those around them, some of the children started to touch the statue. It was bigger than them. One little girl began to caress Mary's face as if to reassure her. Seeing that no one was reprimanding her, the statue was quickly surrounded by curious children anxious to touch the face of Mary. Brought amongst them, it wasn't getting a closer look at the statue which was working, so much as touching her. This art form was working differently now. While I had seen the statue as an aid to our understanding, the children wanted a relationship with her and what she represented. A loving mother worried about her child. Something every child wants.

Making connections

Much of the Bible is focused on the challenge of where we place God in relation to our own human experience. It is very tempting to put God on a shelf in the entrance hall of our lives. If we do so we can control where God features, give nodding assent as we pass by, worship occasionally, and barely encounter the love that is on offer. When Paul preaches to the people of Athens they struggle with the idea that God wants to be close to them. They are used to a God separated from them by plinths and pedestals. A distant God can be worshipped easily enough by dutiful followers.

What might a loving God ask of us? In John's Gospel Jesus invites us into a relationship with his Father. We are called to see ourselves as children of God. If that is not challenging enough, Jesus will call upon the Holy Spirit to help us and that Spirit will reside not in temples or reception areas, but in our hearts. All of this was too much for Athenians who scoffed at Paul's preaching. When God is very near we become afraid of ourselves. Many of us are tempted to rush God back up the ladder, back on the shelf where we can admire from a distance.

Children don't want distance, they want love. Extending their hand out to the statue is a holy longing, a prayer and a desire for connection. We lose this at our peril. John's Gospel is uncompromising on this. God is love, and if we put that love on the shelf it will get dusty and appear to be disapproving of us.

Conversation starters

- Is God on a remote shelf in the background of our lives?
- Why do people fear God coming any closer?

Postscript – the grateful disciple

Suppose it is possible to turn wine into water. Suppose it is possible to lose our sense of joy. One day we wake up to discover we have turned into a sourpuss and a misery. Without ever intending to, we become consumed by lingering and unconscious resentment because life doesn't always give us what we expect. Gratitude can rescue us. In the second volume of this series, *The Grateful Disciple*, you can read how a punctured football, a disruptive class of pupils in Liverpool, a chance meeting in Nottingham Cathedral, a soldier in the trenches, a conversation with a four-year-old about dog poo, a visit to Ellis Island and a tramp who knocked on the door, helped to transform the author's reluctance into gratitude. This is a book for people who feel they are doing their best to keep up, to prove themselves capable, to stay on track, but are beginning to wonder if that is what life is really for. Gratitude is the Christian lens through which to look at life, a disposition which leads to joy. It won't make life easier, but it will make it happier. In this book the author explores why, for those who choose to be followers of Christ, there is the inevitable and gradual emergence of a deeply grateful heart.